THE ESSENTIAL GUIDE TO WRITING WELL
AND
GETTING PUBLISHED

Color-Coded Lessons for Easy Comprehension

* Bonus Feature *

Making Decent Dollars Writing ~ Plus Little-Known
Reward-Reaping Benefits

Robert Banfelder

BB
~~
BROADWATER BOOKS
Riverhead, New York

©2017 Copyright by Robert Banfelder

ALL RIGHTS RESERVED. No part of this book may be reproduced or transmitted in any form by any means, electronic or mechanical, including photocopying and recording or by any information storage and retrieval system, except as may be expressly permitted by the 1976 Copyright Act or in writing from the publisher. Requests for permission should be addressed to:

Broadwater Books
141 Riverside Drive
Riverhead, New York 11901-2451

ISBN: 978-0-9915912-9-9

Printed in the United States of America
10 9 8 7 6 5 4 3 2 1

*For Donna
My partner in life*

Also by Robert Banfelder

FICTION

The Richard Geist Trilogy

Dicky, Richard, and I
The Signing
The Triumvirate

The Justin Barnes Four-Book Series

The Author
The Teacher
Knots
The Good Samaritans

Trace Evidence ~ based on the Robert Shulman serial killer trial

Battered

NONFICTION

The Fishing Smart <u>Anywhere</u> Handbook for Fresh Water & Salt Water

The North American Small & Big Game Hunting Smart Handbook
Bonus Feature: Hunting Africa's & Australia's Most Dangerous Game

Bull's-Eye! The Smart Bowhunter's Handbook ~ Sage Advice on Crossbows, Compound Bows, Broadheads, Targets, Clothing & Gear

ABOUT THE AUTHOR

Robert Banfelder is an award-winning crime-thriller novelist. He holds both a Masters of Arts Degree (genre Creative Writing) and a Bachelor of Arts Degree (Cum Laude) from Queens College of the City University of New York. Banfelder taught college English composition courses, literature, creative writing, poetry, and adult education courses, which he designed. The chairperson of the English Department noted Banfelder as a "gifted teacher."

Bob is an avid outdoorsman and has authored books on fishing and hunting in addition to having written numerous outdoor articles that have appeared in many well-known national and regional publications. Bob is a member of the Outdoor Writers Association of America, New York State Outdoor Writer's Association, and the Long Island Outdoor Communicators Network.

Bob also co-hosts (with Donna Derasmo) an eclectic YouTube Channel: *Special Interests with Bob & Donna*.

Please visit www.robertbanfelder.com for a complete listing of his published works.

TABLE OF CONTENTS

LESSON 1	What's in a Name?	1
LESSON 2	The Art of Writing Fiction & Nonfiction	11
LESSON 3	Structuring the Short Story	20
LESSON 4	Writing Well: Development of a Single Sentence Saying What You Mean	38
LESSON 5	The Art of Fiction & Nonfiction: A Mixed Bag of Tricks	47
LESSON 6	Complexities Concerning Characterization & Plot	59
LESSON 7	Contextual, Grammatical, and Syntactical Problems That Plague Writers ~ Part I AKA "Got any Gum?"	71
LESSON 8	Continued Contextual, Grammatical and Syntactical Problems That Plague Writers ~ Part II	85
LESSON 9	Book Titles and Cover Designs	100
LESSON 10	Organizing Paragraphs for Article Writing	107
LESSON 11	Taking a Spell	122
LESSON 12	Talking It Up — During and After Publication	129
BONUS FEATURE	Making Decent Dollars Writing ~ Plus Little-Known Reward-Reaping Benefits	137

INTRODUCTION

Over the course of many years, college students have come to me with earnest sentiments, statements, and questions referencing writing: "I want to begin a diary," or "I've started a very short story, and I think I can turn it into a novelette or a novella." "I'd like to write a full-length novel." "I want to write for magazines; therefore, how do I break into freelancing articles for money?" "I want to become a journalist." "I want to be a poet." "I simply want to set down a family history for my children to read one day when I'm old and gray or long gone. I've got some amazing stories to tell." "How do I go about writing a blog for bucks?"

Apart from keeping a personal diary, one who wishes to set down a family history in the form of a journal needs to be trained—formally or otherwise—because he or she is inevitably looking to be published. A diary generally differs from a journal in that the former is private (for your eyes only) while the latter is usually meant to be read by others. Addressing genres such as fiction, nonfiction, poetry, even blogging for fun and/or exposure, are for all eyes to view and, yes, critique. As such, you would want to put your best foot forward. To do less would be to trip over your own two feet, shortchanging yourself in the bargain. Most assuredly, you are not going to be taken seriously by those in the industry (literary agents, editors, publishers, et cetera) if you do not know how to write and write well.

Still, there are some folks who will delude themselves into thinking and then firmly believing that there is a more direct route to achieve their goal(s). They eventually realize that alternate paths are made up of detours and dead ends. For example, I have had students who were convinced that they could write like they often think; that is, employing a stream-of-consciousness approach (void of virtually any punctuation and proper syntax), assured that they would get their prose published. It would be highly unlikely that they would see their work professionally published, let alone be paid for it. This random form of writing is generally quite difficult to follow; hence, you will undoubtedly lose your reader (agent, editor, or publisher) whom you will likely be querying. It's the end game before you really even begin. Your very query letter will likely reveal shortcomings if you lack the basic writing skills.

Composing a cover letter and displaying a sample chapter of your work that exhibits run-on sentences, fragments, and comma splices shows a basic lack of skill. Paragraphs that contain the continued use of ambiguous interpretations are doomed to failure. Pages that swing between the poles of reality and fantasy or paragraphs that employ a stream-of-consciousness technique will spell disaster. I can practically promise that you are dead in the water from the onset; you will drown in despair. I would not recommend this approach to a decent writer let alone a neophyte looking to make his or her mark.

If you lack the basic writing skills, or desire to reach beyond your present level of competence, do yourself a big favor and get the required help you need by carefully studying this innovative 12 lesson guidebook. I take the pain out of learning grammar by employing a strikingly unique approach [**color coded for unprecedented clarity and comprehension**]. Too, I'll teach you the tricks and tools of the trade to put you at the top of your writing game. With a Master of Arts degree in English (genre ~ Creative Writing), I was evaluated as a "gifted college instructor" by the chairperson of the English Department. I boast a 98.6% effective rate referencing students having successfully passed the City University of New York (CUNY) Assessment Test in Writing. Additionally, I contributed to earlier editions of *The Random House Guide to Writing*. Full credentials may be viewed on my website: www.robertbanfelder.com.

Enough preaching from the writer's pulpit; you have been warned and wisely advised. Are you ready to proceed with the building blocks for writing well? If so, let's begin in an unintimidating, relaxed fashion. Let's start with the fun aspect of writing; that is, the tools and tricks of the trade. The rest will fall into place quite naturally. Promise.

LESSON 1

What's in a Name?

We'll start by examining characters' names that you choose for your work of fiction. Not every name has to convey something specific; however, your chief characters' given and/or surnames should do exactly that, and for any number of reasons. We'll explore the names that I selected for my hero and heroine, important appellations that I assigned to the two protagonists in my crime thrillers *The Author* and *The Teacher*. You will meet Jackie (Jacqueline) and Justin in Chapter Three of *The Teacher*. But first, allow me to present the problems and pitfalls that I encountered in presenting the manuscript to the publisher and how I overcame these obstacles. They are very important lessons to bear in mind.

Keeping Your Characters' Names in Check

After my novel, *The Teacher*, was perused, accepted for publication, and the contract signed, the editing process soon began. My instructions were to send a batch of no more than twenty pages at a time, which Jean Hackensmith, owner/senior fiction editor of Port Town Publishing, would review with her fine-tooth comb. Jean's major criticism regarding the very first set unfolded like this:

"This is a great scene, Bob—I like Justin already. Heck, I even like Jackie . . . BUT one of the unwritten rules when writing fiction is that no two characters' names should start with the same letter. It gets confusing for the reader. Granted, here one is male, the other female, so confusion would be less likely, but you still might want to *think* about changing one of the names."

Imagine my chagrin in that I felt it was *essential* for me to keep my two protagonists' names, Justin and Jackie, presented as such for the following reasons (which I expanded upon in an e-mail back to my editor):

"Jean, I had given quite a bit of thought in selecting these two characters' names: Justin and Jackie. Too, I thought about the similarity in their given names beginning with the letter **J**. I also felt (as you do in part) that any confusion would be less likely by the mere fact that we're dealing with a male and female team: a black American maverick and a white woman of Sicilian heritage. Furthermore, I packaged them together in that respect, a juxtaposition I feel reinforces Jackie's and Justin's relationship. Jacqueline's (Jackie's) given name has to work on both gender levels; that is, as an androgynous connection, *viewed* by friends and family as an outwardly beautiful, sexy woman, while *known* among her peers as a tough, if not tomboyish covert operative working for law enforcement; namely, the Suffolk County Homicide

Squad. Jacqueline's overt femininity is her weapon; Jackie's thick-skinned underbelly is, paradoxically, a vulnerable milieu—metaphorically as well as literally—as revealed toward the end of the novel.

This leaves us to deal with the name, Justin. Justin is tantamount to justice. Justin and Jackie are, in essence, the *juste-milieux*; that is, the perfect balancing point between two extremes.

In light of these comments, can we both reflect on this? I don't think that Jacqueline (Jackie) or Justin (as referenced) will lead to confusion. If you do, I'll change it. You're the editor, and I'll bow to your discretion.

Too, is there a problem with Dr. James Littleton's name, beginning with the letter **J**?"

Well, my very last question was pretty darn dumb. The editor just got through explaining potential problems with characters' names beginning with the same letter, and then I'm trying to squeeze in another, which had no real justification whatsoever. But Jean was polite and suggested that I change James, as she said:

"As I stated in a previous e-mail, I think you're okay with Justin/Jackie. You pointed out some very good reasons for leaving those characters' names as they are. As for James Littleton, I think I would change the first name there. Just let me know what name you want, and I'll change it in my copy of the first four chapters."

It didn't take me long to realize that I was a **J** junkie, for I had many characters' given names as well as surnames beginning with the letter **J**. Jean quickly pointed out that, "The same rule applies with surnames. No two should start with the same letter." This certainly would lead to the reader's confusion.

Hence, I had a serious problem. I had more characters than there were letters in our alphabet. What to do? Answer. Making a table labeled A through Z, in order to keep track of characters' names, as shown, will save you valuable time and aggravation. Trust me on that. Of course, you will note, for example, that there are, indeed, *five* given names with the same initial letter as referenced in the left-hand box labeled **B**. How do we avoid reader confusion? Along those same lines, how do we get them past a savvy editor—with his or her approval? We do not want the reader distracted or misled. We do want to add variety. Again, what to do?

Within the first **B** box, note that there are two males, two females, along with a nondescript given name. The fact that one is dead by an early chapter, and the others introduced later, avoids confusion. The fact that one is a minor character, while another is merely mentioned, poses no problem at all. The careful spacing of such characters, who share first initial given and surnames will, most certainly, eliminate the possibility of the reader mixing up one character with another.

By utilizing a table as such, you can easily control what could otherwise be a nightmare fraught with chaos and, therefore, confusion. The chart, as illustrated, will help pave the way for name selection. Note that by placing **A**nthony **N**otaro in the left-hand column, then **N**otaro, **A**nthony (et al,) in the right column, I accomplish two things. I keep track and avoid overloading that right-hand column with other surnames beginning with the letter **N**. Next, **N**oel would be a *clear* choice for another character's given name as I've separated the **N**'s between first and last names rather nicely.

THE TEACHER

	GIVEN NAMES		SURNAMES
A	Anthony Notaro, Aaron Goldstein, Alfredo Termotto, Mrs. Antly	A	Alamo, Gloria; Alamo, Wilfredo; Archer: Brian, Kim; Ames, Dr.
B	Billy Baxter, Brian Archer, Brenda Harrison, Bobby Lee, Barbara Cousins	B	Baxter, Billy; Barnes, Justin; Brand, Kate; Booker, Kim (maiden name); Booth, Dr.
C	Clarence Emery, Clifford Giordano, Carla, Carmela Fontana, Clare Yreme	C	Chardavoyne, Mike (alias); Cousins, Tom; Carter, Linda; Cancilla: Phil, Raymond, Dominic (brothers)
D	Desirée Notaro, David Klein, Douglas Oakley, Dale Fulton	D	Dawson, Smitty; Diaz, Inez; Donahue, Ted
E	Ed Willis, Elizabeth Scala, Eugene, Eve Parisi	E	Emery, Clarence; Estrella, José
F	Fred Prescott, Frankie Sunseri, Felix Zamora	F	Fernandes, Octávio; Fernbach, Sarah; Fontana, Carmela
G	Grace Littleton, Gloria Alamo, Gino, Gary York	G	Giordano, Clifford; Groche, Theodore; Goldstein, Aaron
H	Howard Urban, Hector Ramirez, Helen	H	Henris, Lee; Harrison, Brenda; Hendricks; Hawkins, Rufus
I	Ignacio Vasquez, Ileana (Aunt), Inez Diaz	I	Ingrilli, Laura; Idler: Ezekiel (Zeke), Lanelle, Quanah, Quanika
J	Jacqueline (Jackie) Rubino, Justin Barnes, José Estrella	J	Jordon, Dr.
K	Kim Archer, Kate Brand, Kevin McGruder	K	Klein, David; Kilpatrick, Detective; Kerrigan, Detective
L	Lee Henris, Lester Townsend, Linda Carter, Laura Ingrilli, Louis Tempone, Lanelle Idler	L	Littleton: Grace, Timothy, Victoria; Lincoln; Lee, Bobby; Lee, Tang
M	Mike Chardavoyne, Melvyn (Milky) Milken, Monisha Washington, Matty, Mark, Maria, Mary	M	McGruder, Kevin; Mosely; Mills, Robert; Milo, Desirée (maiden name); Monterro; Milken, Melvyn (Milky)

N	Nicholas Notaro, Noel Underwood, Nancy	N	Notaro: Desirée, Anthony, Nicholas
O	Octávio Fernandes, Oliver Sydney, Olivia	O	O'Connor, Ruth; Oakley, Douglas
P	Phil Cancilla, Pam	P	Prescott, Fred; Pratt, Ursula; Pelicano, Theresa; Parisi, Eve
Q	Quanah Idler, Quanika Idler	Q	Quinones, Yolanda
R	Ruth O'Connor, Raymond Cancilla, Robert Mills, Rufus Hawkins	R	Rubino, Jacqueline (Jackie); Rubino, Tomas; Richardson; Ramirez, Hector
S	Smitty Dawson, Sean Donahue, Sarah Fernbach, Susan	S	Sterling, Eve; Sydney, Oliver; Sanchez, Xavier; Scala, Elizabeth
T	Timothy Littleton, Dr.; Tang Lee, Ted Donahue, Theodore Groche, Theresa Pelicano, Tomas Rubino; Tom Cousins	T	Termotto, Alfredo; Tempone, Louis; Townsend, Lester; Taborsky
U	Ursula Pratt, Umberto	U	Urban, Howard; Underwood, Noel
V	Victoria Littleton, Dr.; Victor Cancilla, Vito Vitalo	V	Vazquez, Ignacio; Vitalo, Vito
W	Wilfredo Alamo, Warren	W	Willis, Ed; Whitey (see Hawkins); Washington, Monisha
X	Xavier Sanchez	X	
Y	Yolanda Quinones	Y	York, Gary; Yreme, Clare (alias)
Z	Zena, Zeke (Ezekiel) Idler	Z	Zamora, Felix

In going through the manuscript after Jean's *initial* (pun intended) comments, I thought I would need to put the story in a language that has a more extensive alphabet, for I nearly saturated all of those boxes as you can see—apart from X, Y, and Z. To belabor the point, I was so nonplused and paranoid at having overused the initial letter **J**, I cringed when addressing **J**ean in an e-mail. Hyperbole aside, in all candor, I originally had well over a dozen first and/or last names beginning with the letter **J**: Justin, Jacqueline (Jackie), James, John, Jennifer, Jocelynne, Jean Jennings, Johnson, et cetera. This egregious error was replicated with other letters of the alphabet as well. The model will help the writer avoid such problems. At the same time, in adjacent columns (not shown here), you can expand upon characters' features by keeping track of each; e.g., color of hair and eyes, height, build, so on and so forth.

A word to the wise: Until you can comfortably handle a large number of characters in a work of fiction, do not overload your novel with too many individuals. Otherwise, the work will surely become embedded in a web of confusion. The table that I designed will help keep all your ducks in a row.

And now, let's meet Jackie and Justin, excerpted from chapter three of my award-winning novel *The Teacher*.

The Teacher
Chapter Three [excerpt]

The parking lot at the Bella Sera Restaurant in West Tiana could accommodate well over a hundred vehicles and was almost always filled to capacity for lunch and dinner—seven days a week—from Memorial Day to Labor Day. The three rooms held forty-five tables and seated more than two hundred fifty customers now that the new extension was complete. However, January, February, and most of March were bleak months in the restaurant business in general, and this past winter was no exception.

Jacqueline Rubino, the manager of the restaurant, and Justin Barnes, a source of her irritation at the moment, spoke quietly but animatedly in the back bar area of the expanded premises near closing hour.

Jacqueline shook her dark head emphatically. "No, J. Absolutely and positively no. I don't even understand how you could ask me to do such a thing."

"We did it before," the handsome black man put forth plainly. "Did it for God and country," the six-footer added soberly.

"That's baloney and you know it. You did it for you. *I* did it because Don Ciccio and his people had a stranglehold on my family," the beautiful thin-framed woman affirmed. "I did it for survival, J. My father and uncle didn't work day and night for thirty years in this country so that some gangster could walk in here and take control. I did what I had to do, and that's that. Over and done with. Duty and obligation completed. I'm the manager of this restaurant. Not a murderess."

"I really need you on this one, Jackie. I—"

"No! You're nuts. We were lucky last time. Lucky we're both not sitting in prison for the rest of our lives. I was raised a strict Catholic, Justin. You know my upbringing. You know what I have to live with for the rest of my life. I can only hope that God will forgive me in the end. I ask for His forgiveness every day. I pray for you, too, J. I never told you that, but I do. But if you're hellbent on taking out Clarence Emery, you find yourself someone else or go it alone."

"Jackie, listen to me. Please."

Jacqueline smacked the bottom of an empty carafe firmly upon the black granite countertop. "What do I have to say in order to get through to you? How can you walk in here and ask me to do this, Justin Barnes? Tell me! What right do you have to ask me this? But let me ask you something. Emery's locked up in a mental ward, correct?"

Justin nodded. "Kirby Forensic Psychiatric Center. Ward's Island."

Jacqueline laughed lightly. "Well, I think *you* belong there, fella. Let them handle him. Why do you want to get involved like this? He's finally off the streets."

"For how long?"

"What do you mean for how long? Forever and a day. He'll either receive the death penalty or life in prison without parole. He's not going anywhere."

"Then you really *don't* know him. I know that if I hadn't sent Emery's mentor to the bottom of the sea back then, he'd have somehow surfaced back into society—just like the professor will."

"You don't know that."

"What I know is, if Malcolm Columba were still alive, he'd have found his freedom by now."

"How?"

"The same way Professor Clarence Emery is going to find his."

"How, J?"

"Escape."

"Get real."

"I'm as real as they come, Jackie. And so are you. It's the reason why we're a team."

"Wrong. If you're looking for a team, try coaching Little League, or settle down and find a lasting teammate instead of just stringing that nice girl along. But just leave me the hell alone."

"You know how brilliant and bad this guy is, Jackie."

"I don't care. And you shouldn't care or get involved either. You did enough in dealing with The Author and the others. Let it go and get on with your life."

"This *is* my life, Jackie. When they recruited me, I found real meaning in my life for the first time. A family. A purpose."

"Fine. Then you should know how *I* feel. My family is *my* life, Justin. My husband is the foundation of that life. My purpose is running this place. And you ask me to jeopardize all that?"

Justin ran a large hand atop his nappy pate. "I'm asking you to look beyond one family for a moment and think about many lives, about how many families Emery's already destroyed and about how many more he will destroy before somebody puts him down. That's what I'm asking of you."

"He's locked up, J. He's confined. What do you want me to do? Pay him a visit and put a bullet in his brain, then surrender myself? Huh?"

"What I want you to do is tell me that you'll work with us, and I'll lay it all out for you."

Jacqueline stared at Justin in disbelief. "Do you know why you're still standing there?"

The swarthy man smiled and shook his head.

"Because this is a public place," she said. "That's the only reason. If this were my home, which in a sense it is, I'd ask you to leave. So. There you have it. My answer is no. Now. Do you want something to eat or drink before I change my mind?"

"I thought the kitchen was closed."

"Do you want something to eat or drink?" she repeated.

"Will you just sit down with me and listen?"

"Not a chance."

Justin Barnes shrugged. "He goes absolutely wild over gorgeous Italian girls, Jackie—with the emphasis on wild."

"I'll remind you that I'm a Sicilian woman."

"He's suspected of murdering scores of young women, maybe hundreds, including a female homicide detective. Suddenly, he shows up in New York and gets himself arrested."

"Captured and arrested and now confined."

"All too easy, Jackie. It's nothing more than a little visit. But he'd surely let you pay him a call if we gave him half a reason."

"You're out of line and out of here. Understand?"

"I understand that most of them never saw their twenty-first birthday."

"Then I'll also remind you that I'm thirty-one."

"You don't look a day over nineteen, and you know it."

Jacqueline restrained a smile.

"Gorgeous Mediterranean types he just loves to clock and cut," Justin pushed.

"I just might clock *you* if you don't leave or change the subject."

"Not one of them over a size six."

"Out!"

"That's where *he's* headed, Jackie. Out. I guarantee it."

"*Zu* Phil!"

"Crying uncle's not fair, Jackie," Justin scolded with a smile.

"*Zu* Phil," Jacqueline called again, firmly forming her full lips into an angry frown.

"What happened to that nice sweet girl I knew?"

"Grew up."

Phil Cancilla walked out of the kitchen, drying his hands on a clean white dishtowel before tucking the cloth at the small of his back.

"Hey, J. How are you?"

Justin fondly took the man's hand.

"Fine, Phil. I was just telling Jackie what a fine job she's doing with the place. Not an evening I drive by when the parking lot's not full."

"Well, I been booking a lot of parties lately, otherwise we'd be a little slow this time of year. You hungry? Kitchen's never closed to you, you know."

"Sweet of you, Phil. But I gotta go."

"Full parking lot or not, you stop by anytime, and we'll find a table for you and Ursula. How's she doing?"

"Terrific. Only I wish you or Tomas would give her cooking lessons, and someday soon. I suggested she make fried calamari one evening, and she suggested reservations here."

The owner laughed. "That's a good one."

"He thinks I'm kidding, Jackie. Tell him the face she made when I bought fresh squid from the market."

"Justin was just leaving," Jacqueline said evenly.

"Right. Gotta run. Get to yackin' and I don't know when to shut up."

"Got that right," she said with a smirk.

"Well, take care. And say hello to Tomas and Frankie for me."

"Take care, J." Phil smiled warmly, taking the man's shoulders in for a hug. "And give Ursula our best."

"You bet." Justin turned to her. "Size four if I had to guess," he practically whispered, appreciatively taking in the woman's tall, slim figure. "Ursula is an eight but tells me she's given up fried foods." Addressing them both, he asked, "Hear that joke about squid? Here on the South Shore they call it sushi. Know what they call it over on the North Shore?"

Phil Cancilla shook his head.

"Bait." The black man grinned.

Phil laughed heartily. "Now, that's a *real* good one."

Jacqueline stood fixedly with a stone-cold stare.

"*Bait*, Jackie. Get it?" Justin winked. "Think about it."

"*Ciao*, Justin," she managed, forcing a tight smile.

"Bye, kid."

········

Jackie and Justin . . . . Their given names share a rich alliterative tone; the two are not soon forgotten—or confused. Too, their relationship is a curious juxtaposition of comparisons and contrasts. Again, a *juste-milieux*: the perfect balancing point.

Jackie	Justin
white	black
female	male
Sicilian	Afro-American
androgynous quality to the name; that is, structurally and functionally both female and male: beautiful, feminine ~ soft yet tough (tomboyish)	macho man ~ with a soft side to his inner personality

And that is precisely how I wanted my two characters, Jackie and Justin portrayed. To reiterate the question, What's in a name?

In the *Godfather*, there are striking similarities between novelist Mario Puzo's Johnny Fontaine crooner character and singer Frank Sinatra. One need only explore Miami's Fountainebleau hotel connection where Sinatra performed many a nightclub act, having at one point owned a third of the business.

Consider, too, the scene in the movie where Fontaine approaches his godfather, Don Vito Corleone, eliciting his help in obtaining a role in a movie that would make Johnny Fontaine a big star. However, the Hollywood movie magnate, Jack Woltz, refuses to give Fontaine the role. Hence, the famous line from *The Godfather* as Don Corleone calms his nephew by assuring him that he will, indeed, get the part in the film: "I'm going to make him an offer he can't refuse," says Corleone. The real-life scuttlebutt is that Sinatra's role in *Here to Eternity* was handed to him following mafia involvement with the heads of the studio's production company. True or not, there is sound evidence that Puzo fashioned his character after Ol' Blue Eyes, Frank Sinatra.

In my first novel, *No Stranger Than I* (later republished as *Dicky, Richard, and I*), I name my leading character Richard Geist, fashioned from *Geist*, German for mind, spirit, ghost. The story is a frightening look at madness in the making.

Justin's and Jackie's adversary in my first novel of the Justin Barnes four-book series, *The Author*, is serial killer Malcolm Columba. Mal is a prefix meaning bad. Malcolm is as bad as they come—the personification of evil as are all my serial killer characters.

The antagonist in my second novel of the Justin Barnes four-book series, *The Teacher* (sequel to *The Author*), is Professor Clarence Emery, his given name taken from the Latin word meaning "clear one." As clear thinking as he is diabolical, Clarence Emery is the embodiment of evil and insanity . . . however one wishes to define abnormality.

As I began this guidebook with a caveat in its introduction, I shall continue with a second warning. Please heed the following.

The Teacher went on to become an award-winning novel, and I believed that many copies would soon be printed. Its prequel, *The Author*, also an award-winner, was actually published after *The Teacher*. The reason being that *The Author* was a considerably longer work (initially a two-volume set), and my editor/publisher first wanted to see how *The Teacher* would sell before considering *The Author*. Long story short, Jean Hackensmith of Port Town Publishing folded her tent, declaring bankruptcy after ripping off twenty some odd of her authors, myself included. In the interim, several of us had learned that she had been a convicted felon. I take nothing away from her as an editor; she is good. As a person, she remains a disappointment to many of us.

The lesson to be learned here is to do your due diligence when it comes to seeking an agent, editor, or publisher. A good website is *Absolute Write* at http://www.absolutewrite.com, which hosts a forum where you can research what other writers are saying about specific agents, editors, and publishers. Additionally, agents who are members of The Association of Authors' Representatives are reputable. Unfortunately, the information regarding Port Town Publishing was reported too late by Predators & Editors, a now defunct website. You do the best that you can.

LESSON 2

The Art of Writing Fiction and Nonfiction

A carpenter has a chest full of tangible tools: hammer, saw, screwdriver, file, drill, plane, pliers, et cetera. The implements are, indeed, tactile in that they are handled by a craftsman to create perhaps a cabinet or fashion a fine piece of furniture. A portrait painter, too, has palpable tools: brushes and a palette with which to apply color and form upon a canvas in order to imbue likeness and life. What does a writer have? A writer has his or her own words—words with which to ideally paint a clear picture in one's mind—words that can surely sing and give expression to a work of art. How does a writer accomplish this? Well, a writer also has a trove of tools. Apart from reference books, pen and paper, or a machine to mechanically set down prose—items that can be fingered and felt—a writer's words are otherwise dead to the *literal* sense of touch. Yet, a skillful writer can figuratively make all five senses come alive upon the printed page. This is accomplished through the use of the author's chest of tools. Call it, if you will, our box or bag of tricks.

Let's begin with a tool right now. Reread the above passage, slowly and carefully. Note how certain syllables and words flow together. Focus on the words beginning with the letter c, t, f, p, l, m, and b. Observe how they are connected in the following phrases: *t*angible *t*ools; *c*raftsman to *c*reate; *f*ashion a *f*ine piece of *f*urniture; *p*ortrait *p*ainter . . . *p*alpable . . . *p*alette; *l*ikeness and *l*ife; *t*rove of *t*ools, *m*achine to *m*echanically; *f*ingered and *f*elt; *p*rinted *p*age, *b*ox or *b*ag. Aside from such common expressions as 'portrait painter' and 'printed page,' ask yourself if the other articulations are coincidental. Be assured that they are not.

The words and/or phrases are *f*ashioned to *f*low u*p*on the *p*age just as surely as I am a*p*plying emphasized *p*rose here. This device is referred to as **alliteration**. The technique can be quite powerful if employed correctly. Note that in this very example, the repetitive letters (which are italicized here as well as above) are solely for the purposes of instruction and need not necessarily appear at the beginning of each word but can also function as words with the same <u>stressed</u> initial <u>consonant</u> sound(s).

"*C*old *o*ld bones lie *o*n the b*o*ttom *o*f the sea," is such an example. The stressed initial <u>vowel</u> sound is the letter o. Read this line aloud to feel the doom. That is precisely what the author is striving to attain.

"Better buy Bond Bread because Bond Bread builds better bodies," is an obvious example of stressed initial sound appearing as the first letter in each word. The bread company believed that their catchy alliterative slogan would stay in the minds of their customers and prospective customers. And it worked! I remember that catch phrase from the fifties to this very day. Whenever I went to the store for my mom to pick up white bread, I'd come home with a loaf of Bond Bread.

Once new writers latch on to this technique, the tendency is to overuse it. If this literary technique is handled subtly, as I believe it was in my opening paragraph, in that I probably had to literally point the plotted language out to you, then you, too, can successfully pull this off. Try to avoid being heavy-handed. Conversely, when employed for obvious emphasis as in the Bond Bread example, use the method sparingly.

Under the umbrella of alliteration are two forms: **assonance** and **consonance**.

Assonance stresses <u>vowel</u> sounds as the letter o in "C*o*ld *o*ld b*o*nes lie *o*n the b*o*ttom *o*f the sea."

Consonance stresses <u>consonant</u> sounds as the letter b in "Better buy Bond Bread because Bond Bread builds better bodies."

You can set and control a mood by paying close attention to assonant and consonant tones.

Let's examine the opening chapter in *The Teacher*. The first paragraph is fraught with alliteration. Without my signaling those words and phrases, read the following and see what you can pick up on your own—now that your antenna is up and positioned properly. Don't dwell or concern yourself with questionable alliterative words and phrases, only those that stand out and grab you.

Let's meet Grace Littleton.

The Teacher
Chapter One [excerpt]

With thin wrists firmly secured behind a scrawny back, her head and body locked solidly in place within a wooden makeshift vise, Grace Littleton lay face down on a sheet of Lucite, naked and shivering, although the building was sufficiently heated. The serial killer's caged and spiritless songbird hung silent upon her stationary swing—a scaffold suspended in a vaulted ceiling, seventy-seven feet from dome to doom. Between two planks spaced but a pinkie finger's width apart, San Francisco's opera star could certainly see but not cry out to the work crew cutting and laying a stone tile floor far below her. Wide strips of duct tape smacked across the singer's malleable mouth made her doubtlessly mute. The monotonous and interminable sound of several grating ceiling fans muffled any sob, moan or groan she might emit.

·······

Although there are several examples of alliteration in the above paragraph, the fourth, fifth, and sixth lines should have popped up upon the page: The serial killer's caged and spiritless songbird hung silent upon her stationary swing—a scaffold suspended in a vaulted ceiling, seventy-seven feet from dome to doom. The *s*'s and

d's have surely sounded in your ear, especially if read aloud. Read silently, the powerful passage still possesses a subliminal effect. The ***s***'s and ***m***'s in the next to the last sentence should have grabbed your attention, too. Wide strips of duct tape smacked across the singer's malleable mouth made her doubtlessly mute.

Once again, there are other examples of alliteration in this paragraph; however, if you picked up on the two samples cited, your antenna is working just fine and you have absorbed this lesson well. Congratulations.

To add another dimension to this exercise, be aware that such wording as [***p***hrases ***f***ound] has the same stressed initial sound, yet the words do not share the same letter. Still, this is a definite form of alliteration.

All right, let's move on to other literary devices in our trove of tricks: **comparisons**. The first and simplest is the **simile**. A simile is a figure of speech employing a comparison between two dissimilar objects or ideas yet makes clear their connection. The words *as*, *like*, and *than* are used to connect them. Here are examples of each.

He slithers *like* a snake.
He seemed tough *as* nails.
The group grew wilder *than* a tornado in a trailer park.

Note, too, the overlap referencing alliteration in the first sentence: He ***s***lithers like a ***s***nake. The ***s***'s form the consonant sounds and practically hiss at you.

Also, discern the ***g***'s and ***t***'s in the third sentence: The ***g***roup ***g***rew wilder than a ***t***ornado in a ***t***railer park.

Are pictures not being formed in your mind? Are the words of the writer not clearly depicting those pictures? You bet they are.

Let's examine a couple of examples of similes by lifting several lines from *The Teacher*. First, allow me to set the scene. Clarence Emery, my antagonist, is restrained in a straitjacket, seated across from Doctor Timothy Littleton, the director of Kirby Forensic Psychiatric Center on Ward's Island, situated on the East River, two-thirds of a mile east of Manhattan.

The Teacher
Chapter Two [excerpt]

"I'd like to keep this dialogue close to home, Clarence. I'd like to—"
"Fine. First off, I don't see as how we're engaging in any sort of dialogue. More of a monologue, I'm sure you realize. I'm trying to avoid a tirade here, which is kind of difficult when you just sit there like a zombie in a trance. Close to home, you say? All right. We'll talk about the nuns here on our soil who are getting abused and raped as well. But I want input, Timmy. To use your word, I, too, wish to establish a dialogue. You see, I want to learn as much about you as you wish to learn about me."
The psychiatrist smiled.

Note the simile in the sentence printed in red. The psychiatrist is seated across from his patient "*like* a zombie in a trance."

During the same session between the psychiatrist and his patient, we find a more elaborate simile.

Doctor Littleton picked up his pen. "Clarence…"

"Yes, Timmy?"

"How was it that you came to take the lives of those two young women in a parking area at Pipes Cove in Greenport?"

Clarence shook his head sadly. "Sorry, Timmy. It's just not that cut-and-dried. It's a matter of degrees. You would first have to evaluate each and every facet like so many marks on the rim of a compass card if you're to fully and truly understand. For there are many ranges of reference you'd have to explore in order to chart the course of my actions. I'm trying to head you in a given direction if you'll let me. We can start or end with littering or loitering or lobbying. Anywhere you like. But we must come full circle. Then and only then will you understand madness in the making." Emery raised his eyes to the diplomas along the wall. "Those degrees, Timmy? Just forget about everything you ever learned in school. Not applicable, here. Understand?"

Doctor Littleton stared silently at his obstreperous patient.

Note not only the sentence in red containing the simile, but those words and phrases that come before, during, and after the comparison; words and phrases that relate to a compass: 'degrees,' 'facet,' 'marks on the rim of a compass card,' 'ranges of reference,' 'chart a course,' 'head you in a given direction,' 'full circle'.

Yes, I do believe that you're getting the <u>drift</u> . . . pun intended.

Our next form of comparison is the **metaphor**. Simply put, a metaphor is a figure of speech that *suggests* a similarity between two objects or ideas. Sometimes it requires a bit of brain power to make the connection. The connection may not be as obvious as a simile. In the example, "A mighty fortress is our God," the two elements being compared are clearly fortress and God. God protects us *like* a fortress affords protection. (Note that we have converted a metaphor to a simile through the use of the word *like*.) However, in the next sampling, ask yourself what is being compared to what? "The ship plows through the sea." Is the ship being *compared* to the sea? Think hard. Or is the ship being compared to a plow? Without thinking carefully, one might answer ship and sea because they both function as nouns [persons, places, or things] in this sentence while the plow functions as a verb. Yet, it is the ship that is being compared to the plow in the sense that a large oceangoing vessel cuts through the sea much like a plow cuts through (tills) the earth. It takes great force to accomplish either feat. Now, let's hear that sentence aloud with a bit of emphasis. "The ship *plows* through the sea." Say it aloud and accentuate the *p*. The ship *plows* through the sea. The *p* functions as a plosive; feel its power. Let it explode from your mouth. That is what the writer wants you to *see* and *hear*.

In the classroom, I insert a forefinger into the corner of my mouth and make a loud popping sound to emphasize both the power of the plow and ship cutting through earth and sea, respectively. The image and sound created stays in students' minds and helps reinforce the lesson.

Excerpted from the opening paragraph in the prologue of my first novel, *Dicky, Richard, and I* (originally published as *No Stranger Than I*), I want to draw your attention to the second sentence.

Dicky, Richard, and I
Prologue [excerpt]

North Shore State Hospital
for the Criminally Insane
Havenwood, Long Island, New York
1969

The eighteen-year-old boy lie semiconscious, badly beaten and bleeding, strapped to a hospital bed. A river of red spilled freely from his mouth as four male attendants entered the room. Coal-black faces contrasted sharply against bloodied white sheets and walls as the patient's sea-green eyes danced insanely in his head. Suddenly, the duty nurse burst into the room and over to the patient's bed.

"My God! He's bitten off his tongue," Nurse Crayford exclaimed, exploring the rictus wide.

On a figurative level, the phrase, river of red, makes clear that we are *seeing* a river of blood running from the boy's mouth. Metaphorically, we are comparing images of a great amount (a river) of (red) blood being spilled.

On a literal level, the words river of red could pertain to a *river* passing through an area where the earth is rich in *red* clay or soil, the waters taking on that color. A biblical reference points to the kingdom of Sennaar, a territory at the confluence of the great Nile and the Nile of Abyssinia ". . . the soil of which is a red bole, becomes colored with that earth."

Note, too, that the metaphor, river of red, is also alliterative, employing consonance through the letter r. Perhaps a bit of a stretch—perhaps not—can you feel (now that your antenna is up) the 'river of red' running or rushing . . . if not as exampled in my novel, then perchance at the confluence of the great Nile and the Nile of Abyssinia?

My point here is that a metaphor can be a simple or complicated comparison. In any regard, it is a powerful tool. As a matter of fact, consider it your power tool with which to cut and shape fine images.

Excerpted from a later chapter in *Dicky, Richard, and I*, patient Richard Geist, confined to the King Foundation, a low-security private mental institution, interacts with another patient.

Dicky, Richard, and I
Chapter 12 [excerpt]

PATIENTS AND PATIENCE

Richard stood just inside the sparse but immaculate room while Mrs. Ackerman went on to explain why she alone stood closer to God, confident in the fact that it was she who occupied a space at the very top of B Building, whereas her good friend, Mrs. Alvarez, was confined to the second floor, thereby concluding that the Spanish woman was several levels beneath her in station as well. Mrs. Ackerman avowed that she alone would be the first to serve God.

In the above example, the physical location of Mrs. Ackerman's room in relationship to how she perceives God watching over her is a metaphor. It compares an object or thing (in this case her <u>room</u>) with a <u>belief</u>: the conviction that God is observing Mrs. Ackerman from above while her good friend Mrs. Alvarez is confined to a room several floors below. Mrs. Ackerman's proximity to God is, in her mind's eye, indeed, comforting to the woman.

For our last comparison, we will explore the **analogy**. I don't mean a likeness explained away in a simple phrase or even a single sentence as we covered by way of the simile and metaphor, but rather by employing a more intensified technique; a mode or model from which to connect two seemingly unlike objects, ideas, entities— et cetera. The analogy I am about to unfold before you shall require a good many words in order to make the connection, and then to reinforce it through example. Let's begin by comparing a person to a car, excerpted from Richard Schickel's review of *Patriot Games* in *Time* magazine. Apart from careless writing, that is, the reviewer's splitting the word 'time span' [sic] (which is a compound word: timespan), then beginning one sentence with And, another with But, both in the same paragraph, the analogy is not half bad.

"Harrison Ford is like one of those sports cars that advertise acceleration from 0 to 60 m.p.h. in three or four seconds. He can go from slightly broody inaction to ferocious reaction in approximately the same time span. And he handles the tight turns and corkscrew twists of a suspense story without losing his balance or leaving skid marks on the film. But maybe the best and most interesting thing about him is that he doesn't look particularly sleek, quick, or powerful; until something or somebody causes him to gun his engine, he projects the seemly aura of the family sedan."

In Schickel's first sentence, a simile applying the word *like* is used to make the person/car comparison: "Harrison Ford is like one of those sports cars . . . ." Through the use of language pertaining to automobiles, especially high-performance machines, Schickel immediately expands the connection. "0 to 60 m.p.h. in three or four seconds," "tight turns," "corkscrew twists," "skid marks," "sleek, quick, or powerful," and "gun his engine." Schickel has neatly wrapped up those similarities by *showing us*, not just by telling us, that Harrison Ford can switch between a somewhat gloomy mild-mannered performance and fierce character portrayal just as suddenly as a high-performance vehicle can accelerate and maneuver. The juxtaposition of "the family sedan" and a "sports car" in comparing the actor's ability to quickly switch gears is, indeed, powerful. I just had to add my own two cents worth in order to show that you could certainly expand upon this mode of comparison.

Let's examine an analogy that I introduce in the college classroom, lecture hall, or through informal discussions. Upon first glimpse, it appears that there is little if anything that a church and a neighborhood bar have in common. I make it clear that when I refer to a church, I am referring to our places of worship regardless of denomination.

"Would you agree that a church and a neighborhood bar have little if anything in common?" I bait the audience. Most everyone agrees, until I have them sit back and take a moment to *think* about their house of worship and the local watering hole. Men, women, and young adults begin brainstorming comparisons. Hands suddenly go up, and the discussion begins. Usually, the first connection that a class or an audience makes between a church and a bar is that both buildings are places where people gather or *congregate*—an assemblage of folks who *flock* as a group for a common purpose. When asked what that purpose might be, invariably everyone agrees that it comes down to people taking refuge from the problems of everyday life. While there may be many reasons why people attend church or patronize a barroom, the fact remains that the commonality they share is that both establishments offer a form of social solace, that is, a feeling of belonging and comfort.

Respective of the church and the local gin mill, I then ask who its members and customers take note of specifically. In other words, who is running the show at these respective locations? I serve only in the capacity of a facilitator, leading the group in a general direction, not answering any questions, but simply raising them. It is important that the group makes the connection for itself.

"Who is in charge and *serves* in both a literal and figurative sense?" I press.

"The priest," declares an elderly woman seated before me in the front row.

"The bartender," answers a young man in the back of the auditorium.

"The rabbi," remarks a teenage boy, finding a seat.

"What exactly do they *serve*?" my question begs.

"Alcohol."

"Sermons."

"Wine poured into the chalice," a young girl whispers excitedly.

"Both the bartender and Father O'Brian serve as good listeners," emphatically states another neighborhood teenager.

"Oh, yeah? Father O'Brian left the parish four years ago, which tells us the last time you've been to church, Tommy," his friend seated next to him teases good-naturedly.

The crowd is on a roll.

Next, I ask the assembled group if there is any *parallel* that can be drawn between where the bartender serves and the ecclesiastical leader performs religious rites. A multitude of hands rise to the heavens.

I call on the girl who whispered with regard to wine being poured into a chalice.

"The bar counter could be compared to an altar," she states magnificently.

"Where the priest serves wine and bread," another adds.

"Like the bartender places bowls of pretzels and potato chips on the counter and pours wine and beer, serving his customers," a man in a wheelchair elaborates.

I smile and nod approval. "Great. You're forming a nice *analogy*," I say to all of them. "Behind that countertop, directly in back of the bartender, stands what?" I continue with questions.

"Bottles of booze!" a man exclaims.

"And those bottles of booze are being *reflected* by . . . ?" I let the question hang there.

"A mirror," a voice from the rear reasons immediately.

"Good. Now, let's see how many boozers we have with us this afternoon," I challenge teasingly. "Tell me not only the colors that you see reflected in that mirror, but what they represent."

"Browns for whiskeys, ryes, and brandies," was the first reply.

"Ah, I just knew I could count on at least one boozer in the group," I declared. No one in the audience wants to be left out of the mix.

"Red wine."

"A very light reddish color wine—like rosé."

"A darker red ruby wine. Cabernet Sauvignon."

"Amber colored beers."

"Green for crème de menthe."

"Godiva white chocolate liqueur," a young lady expressed deliciously, smacking her lips for the full effect.

"What's that tall, phallic-shaped bottle of yellow liqueur called?" an elderly lady demands of the gentleman sitting beside her.

"Wishful thinking," remarks her husband.

The audience is practically rolling in the aisles.

"Galliano," a middle-aged Italian gentleman answered from his seat when the place finally calmed down to the point where he could be heard above continued laughter. "The liqueur is Galliano."

"That's it!" the woman who raised the question said with satisfaction. "Galliano."

"There is also a blue liqueur called Curaçao," a Spanish woman explained, "traditionally made from the peels of Valencia oranges, known as larahas, produced on the island of Curaçao in the Caribbean." The woman started to launch into her family history, and a man from Venezuela swore that the liqueur was orange in color, not blue.

In order to clear up the confusion and get the man back on track, I explained that when naturally produced, the liqueur is colorless and that often artificial coloring is added—most commonly blue or orange. Also, I had to politely bring the woman's attention back to the point of our discussion.

"All right, by stretching our imaginations a bit, can we connect all those colors—the browns, and reds, amber, green, white, yellow, blue and orange—from the reflected bottles seen in the bartender's mirror, to something familiar that we find in the church?"

There is a moment of hesitation before it hit home.

"Stained-glass windows!" someone bellows from the back of the auditorium.

"There you go," I announce and applaud the group as a whole. "That was well-done, ladies and gentlemen and boys and girls. Give yourselves a well-deserved hand."

The group nods knowingly, and the clapping continues. They are very pleased with themselves.

"You can see how it took more than just a few words to make our comparisons between a church and a bar," I remind them. "You are now on your way to creating your own analogies between seemingly dissimilar entities."

LESSON 3

Structuring the Short Story

Before an aspiring author begins a story, it would be wise to understand narrative structure. *The Lottery*, a short story written by Shirley Jackson, published in 1948, is a wonderful piece of literature with which to illustrate certain techniques. They will serve as additional implements for the storyteller to add to his or her trove of tools. In order to receive the full benefit of this lesson, I would like for you to follow my directions as described.

In the classroom, I initially start out by having students read only the first and last sentence of *The Lottery*, ostensibly ruining the story by having revealed its ending. I make no apologies. This approach has a sudden impact on the class. Why should this day be different than any other? As we eventually read through the narrative, which runs approximately five-and-a-half pages, you will see lessons resurface. This will serve as reinforcement. Too, you will learn new methods and modes concerning style and structure before mastering and making them your own.

On completion of this short story, I'm certain you will agree that *The Lottery* is truly a classic—a real eye-opener, for you will see precisely *why* the piece is priceless. Let's begin by reading only the first and last sentence of this short story before going any further. You need not hunt down a copy of *The Lottery*, which is presented in its entirety at the end of this lesson. However, for openers, I only want you to read and examine the first and last sentence. I have presented those two sentences forthwith.

1st sentence:

The morning of June 27th was clear and sunny, with the fresh warmth of a full-summer day; the flowers were blossoming profusely and the grass was richly green.

Last sentence:

"It isn't fair, it isn't right," Mrs. Hutchinson screamed, and then they were upon her.

I'm sure you are questioning what is going on here. I'm certain that we are all in agreement that the first sentence is absolutely positive, whereas the final sentence of the story is positively negative. However, this order of structuring is not written in stone, for the story could begin negatively and end on a positive note. Conversely, as already noted here, the piece began in a positive light and ended negatively.

Next, let's examine the very title itself: *The Lottery*. Does it suggest a positive or negative feeling? When we think of a lottery, I'm sure a few questions come to mind. What am I going to *win*? What kind of a *chance* do I have to realize a *prize*? A lottery implies some sort of possible gain, generally thought to be positive. But what if it had an opposite effect? What if when you *win*, you actually *lose*? What if when you are the winner of the lottery, you pay the ultimate price? Your life!

That is precisely Shirley Jackson's neat little twist as the author clearly reveals the outcome in her final sentence:

"It isn't fair, it isn't right," Mrs. Hutchinson screamed, and then they were upon her.

Mrs. Hutchinson is about to lose her life.

Rest assured that there will be several indications along the telling that all is not well with winning the lottery. Be sure, too, (once your antenna is up and properly tuned) that there will be more than a few hints that winning the lottery does not sit well with most folks of this rural town. These telltale signs will become quite evident as you become well-versed in the reading of literary signposts. First, let's deal with the **irony** found in the title, especially when coupled to those first and last sentences.

The mere **title**, *The Lottery*, communicates something positive.

The very first sentence conveys positive feelings through the use of such words, phrases and images that paint a clear and warm, sunny summer June morning, with an array of colorful flowers exploding before a richly green backdrop:

1st sentence:

The morning of June 27th was clear and sunny, with the fresh warmth of a full-summer day; the flowers were blossoming profusely and the grass was richly green.

The last sentence certainly leaves one with the impression of doom looming over Mrs. Hutchinson, by the author having employed such words, phrases, and images that create the feeling of apprehension if not downright dread.

Last sentence:

"It isn't fair, it isn't right," Mrs. Hutchinson screamed, and then they were upon her.

Throughout a portion of this chapter, I'll keep the author's prose colored in teal. However, to clarify literary examples, I'll employ underlining and *italics* in order to bring to your attention and emphasize the elements of **symbolism** and **dramatic irony**.

What you see and expect from the title and the first sentence of *The Lottery* is not at all what you receive in reading the last sentence. You are thrown a curve. There is incongruity between what might be expected and what actually occurs. This is an example of **irony** and an important technique to employ in structuring a story. Consider it a valuable tool to add to your treasure chest of implements.

Let's begin to move through the narrative and catch the writer's drift. You may pause here and first read the story for yourself, or you may continue as I highlight and discuss significant elements. The choice is yours. Just be sure not to skip a beat, or you will severely shortchange yourself.

In the second rather lengthy sentence of *The Lottery*, we learn that in some towns the lottery took two days to complete because there was such a large population, whereas in this village of about 300 people, the lottery was over in less than a couple of hours. Nothing unusual at this point; however, later in the piece, I'll return your attention to this sentence in the sense of town versus village. Remember, our antennae are up, and we are looking for trouble because the positive aspect of *this* particular lottery is not what it initially appears to be.

In the second paragraph, there is a hint that something might be amiss. Referencing the schoolchildren, "the feeling of liberty sat uneasily on most of them." Ask yourself why *uneasily*, especially in light of the fact that school is over for the summer. Next, your attention is directed to the boys' pockets full of stones, and a moment later to a great pile of stones gathered by two boys, one whose name is Dickie Delacroix, whom the author tells us the villagers pronounced Dellacroy. Why in the world would Shirley Jackson bother to tell us that? A good writer does not waste words. A skillful author does not use filler to expand the page. A successful writer strives to achieve compactness of prose. Again, why is Jackson going on about the surname Delacroix, pronounced Dellacroy? Hold that thought in abeyance as we move ahead to the last sentence in that paragraph, lifting the phrase, "and the very small children rolled in the dust . . . ." Dust is a universal **literary symbol** representing death and/or decay. In literature, it is a signal for you to tune that antenna. It is a **foreshadowing** of foreboding events to follow. Stay focused when you are dealing with *dust*.

Back to the name Dickie Delacroix. Remember our first lesson? What's in a name? In *The Lottery*, the names that we are initially introduced to, both given and surnames, are Bobby Martin and Bobby and Harry Jones. They are common American names, names that represent a solid American background. Other such names will follow; for example, Mr. Summers, Mr. Graves, Mr. Adams, Mr. Warner, the Dunbars, and the Hutchinson family. Yet, Shirley Jackson is telling us that the villagers have taken the trouble to Americanize Delacroix, pronouncing it Dellacroy. Croix is French for cross, another **symbol** to be examined closely.

Also, look at three of the surnames in a different light: Graves, Adams, and Warner.

Could we be accused of overreaching at this early point in the story by suggesting that the story has biblical overtones after noting such words as stones, dust, cross, and Adams? Perhaps. Could we be accused of overreaching by suggesting that its tone is ominous or evil? We already know the ending, at least in part. However, we would need further examples throughout the story to support such direful contentions. For the moment, let's isolate and list some of the key words that might lead us to such conclusions:

a pile of stones
dust
cross

Next, let's isolate, list, and examine parts of those surnames.

Delacroix (cross)
Graves (grave ~ a place of burial)
Adams (Adam ~ first man)
Warner (warn) or Warner (war)

Is this a grave situation that we're dealing with concerning *The Lottery*? Is there a warning or sort of mini-war being waged of which we should be aware? Does Mr. Adams symbolize the first man? Are these elements serendipitous (accidental), or is Shirley Jackson's short story being carefully crafted—working on both a literal and figurative level? Let's jump to the end of the story and read the last six sentences, which will help answer some of these questions:

Tessie Hutchinson was in the center of a cleared space by now, and she held her hands out desperately as the villagers moved in on her. "It isn't fair," she said. A stone hit her on the side of the head.
  Old Man Warner was saying, "Come on, come on, everyone." Steve Adams was in the front of the crowd of villagers, with Mrs. Graves beside him.
  "It isn't fair, it isn't right," Mrs. Hutchinson screamed, and then they were upon her.

As stoning constituted a form of punishment in the Bible, I feel you would agree that at this juncture there are, indeed, biblical overtones concerning *The Lottery*. Be reminded of Jesus addressing a group that was about to stone an adulteress: "He that is without sin among you, let him first cast a stone at her." (John 8:7, King James Version)
The situation in this village is, indeed, grave.
Let's return to the beginning and examine the third paragraph where we learn that the men are talking about planting, rain, tractors, and taxes, joking quietly, smiling rather than laughing, the author informs us. The women appear in faded housedresses. Mention of the pile of stones is twice addressed in this paragraph. Shirley Jackson is

subtly setting the stage for us.

In the fourth paragraph, we meet a seemingly altruistic gentleman, Mr. Summers, a round-faced jovial man who runs a <u>coal</u> business, gratuitously giving his time to the village's civic programs: positive social activities such as square dances, the teenage club, and the Halloween program. He arrives at the square, where the lottery is to be conducted, carrying a <u>black wooden box</u>. Are these **symbols** beginning to form a bleak picture in your mind?

Mr. Graves, carrying a three-legged stool, follows Mr. Summers to where the stool is placed in the center of the square. Mr. Summers sets the <u>black box</u> down upon the stool. The villagers keep their distance, and when asked by Mr. Summers to lend a hand, there is *hesitation* before a father and son come forward to hold the box steady upon the stool while Mr. Summers stirs the <u>papers</u> within the <u>box</u>.

In the fifth paragraph, we learn that the lottery has been going on for generations, steeped in tradition, predating Old Man Warner, the oldest man in the village. <u>The black box</u>, allegedly constructed from an older box, grew shoddier each year, <u>splintered</u>, <u>faded,</u> and <u>stained</u>. Since we already know the final judgment, in that Tessie Hutchinson is sure to die at the end of this story, the <u>black box</u> **symbolizes** a <u>miniature coffin</u>.

The <u>black box</u>, inasmuch as it contains the slips of <u>paper</u> for the drawing, at this point, we can safely surmise that if you *win* the lottery, in essence, you *lose*—your life! Therefore, those slips of <u>paper</u> **symbolize** an *ephemeral existence*, for once a year a villager is sure to succumb as a result of the ill-conceived lottery. That person's life will be cut short by the other villagers as they stone the unlucky victim to death, evidenced in the last line of the story:

"It isn't fair, it isn't right," Mrs. Hutchinson screamed, and then they were upon her.

Hence, powerful **ironies** become clearly evident by the conclusion of the story. The very title, *The Lottery*, is anything but positive as generally thought. Also, the **juxtaposition** (the examination of two or more elements set side by side for the sake of comparing and/or contrasting) of those first and last sentences is totally incongruous. Shirley Jackson has set us up nicely for the fall from our senses. We see the opposite of what we would expect from a lottery. In the end, we witness *death* at a barren village square instead of *life* backdropped against a flowery and rich green landscape as seen in the beginning of the story.

In paragraph seven, we learned that most of the formality concerning the lottery has been lost or put aside over the course of years. Yet, Mr. Summers, as well as like-minds, has successfully managed to keep the tradition alive.

Because we know the ending, additional **irony** can be appreciated in paragraph eight. Tessie Hutchinson hurries along the path to the square because she is practically late:

> Mrs. Hutchinson came hurriedly along the path to the square, her sweater thrown over her shoulders, and slid into place in the back of the crowd. "Clean forgot what day it was," she said to Mrs. Delacroix, who stood next to her, and they both laughed softly. "Thought my old man was out back stacking wood," Mrs. Hutchinson went on, "and then I looked out the window and the kids was gone, and then I remembered it was the twenty-seventh and came a-running." She dried her hands on her apron, and Mrs. Delacroix said, "You're in time, though. They're still talking away up there."

What is Mrs. Hutchinson nearly late for? The **irony** is that she is almost late for her own clichéd <u>funeral</u>. But as Mrs. Delacroix says, "You're in time, though...." The expanded **irony** is that Tessie Hutchinson is in time for her own <u>death warrant</u>, soon to be handed down in a matter of speaking.

The **irony** continues in paragraph nine as Tessie Hutchinson "tapped Mrs. Delacroix on the arm as a *farewell* . . . " [another prefiguring or **foreshadowing**]. Mr. Summers adds to its double meaning by stating, "Thought we were going to have to get on without you, Tessie." Had we not first taken a peek at the ending of the story or, better yet, had our antennae raised in order to tune into these literary tools of **dramatic irony** and **literary symbolism** employed by the author's clever crafting of narrative, we might not initially come to fully appreciate the construction of Jackson's work on this far deeper level—unless, of course, we're well-versed in interpreting literary signposts.

However, there is the danger for readers to now suddenly see and read into things that may not be there. How can we tell if we are interpreting such symbols and irony correctly? The answer is that the interpretations must be legitimately supported by continued emphasis and repetitiveness throughout the context of the story. As we move through this piece, I'm sure you'll agree that Shirley Jackson does exactly that.

At this point in the story, let me draw your attention to the characters themselves, revealed mostly through dialogue rather than presented via the voice of the **omniscient narrator** (all-knowing, third-person recounting). There tends to be a flatness of characterization, meaning that there is no real depth or individuality imbued into the people we meet. The villagers simply symbolize abstract qualities. Pure detachment and objectivity typify the author's treatment of her characters. It is also at this juncture that we learn of a reluctance to partake in the drawing of the lottery as the event gets under way, such as when Mrs. Dunbar is asked to fill in for her husband because of her son's age: "Horace's not but sixteen yet," Mrs. Dunbar said *regretfully*. "Guess I gotta fill in for the old man this year," or when the Watson boy "blinked his eyes *nervously*" because he has to draw for his mother and himself.

The drawing is under way as Mr. Summers is about to read the names of the heads of families, at which point the men (the exception being Janey Dunbar), one at a time, will step forward and take a folded paper from the box until all the slips have been selected. Steve <u>Adams</u> is the <u>first man</u> to be called. Both he and Joe Summers grin at one another humorously and nervously. Alphabetically, Mr. Summers summons forward the heads of the families, each person withdrawing a folded slip of paper.

In the background, Mrs. Delacroix and Mrs. Graves converse:

Seems like there's no time at all between lotteries anymore," Mrs. Delacroix [symbol for cross] said to Mrs. Graves in the back row. "Seems like we got through with the last one only last week."

"Time sure goes fast," Mrs. Graves [place of burial] said.

Next, Mr. <u>Graves</u> goes forward and greets Mr. Summers <u>gravely</u>. Here, via a **pun** (a play on words), Shirley Jackson is emphasizing her point. I trust you'll note that the underlined and/or italicized words elicited throughout the narrative support such dominant themes as Death by Chance, Man's Inhumanity to his Fellow Man, and the Meaninglessness of Life in such a situation as presented in *The Lottery*. Are not these **motifs** (dominant themes) hammered away over and over again by way of continued emphasis and repetitiveness throughout the context of the story?

We are up to the H's when Bill Hutchinson's name is called:

"Get up there, Bill," Mrs. Hutchinson said, and the people near her laughed.

The obvious **irony**, here, is that Bill Hutchinson's wife, Tessie Hutchinson, is expediting her own death sentence by hurrying her husband.

A moment later, a conversation between Mr. Adams and Old Man Warner ensues. Mr. Adams says, "They do say that over in the north village they're talking of giving up the lottery." It becomes immediately clear via Old Man Warner's retort that he is a powerful voice behind keeping the tradition of the lottery alive, denouncing the young folks for failing to uphold the customs passed on from generation to generation. Embedded in his harangue is a strong hint that forms the basis of *why* neighboring towns and villages hold a lottery in the first place, continuing for decades: "Lottery in June, corn be heavy soon." Old Man Warner is clearly equating the annual sacrifice of a human being to a good harvest. In other words, if the villagers did not conduct the lottery and sacrifice someone annually, there wouldn't be a good crop. "First thing you know, we'd all be eating stewed chickweed and acorns. There's *always* been a lottery," the old man states rather irritably.

Old Man Warner's reference to the young folks living in caves and not working anymore **ironically** suggests an <u>uncivilized</u> existence. Yet, it is the village hierarchy that is fostering that very behavior: individuals such as Mr. Summers, who runs a <u>coal</u> business; Mr. Graves, the postmaster; and, of course, Old Man Warner—the oldest man in the village. As we already know the conclusion, we begin to note additional irony. The annual <u>sacrifice</u> is tantamount to <u>murder</u>, although Old Man Warner doesn't see it that way, calling the young folks "a pack of crazy fools," even complaining about "Joe Summers up there joking with everybody." Old Man Warner has seen tradition slipping away through the years; he is, in effect, losing control.

It is interesting to note that after seventy-seven years, Old Man Warner has somehow, *luckily*, managed to avoid drawing the *winning* slip of paper, which perhaps raises the question as to whether this is a rigged game among the elders within the hierarchy. Regardless, we can appreciate the **irony** in that the gathering and grouping of families before the village square eventually results in a *break* among family members.

Finally, all the names of heads of households have been called—**A** through **Z**. Those holding their folded slips of paper open them *apprehensively*, thereby narrowing the eventual *winner* down to one family before a single member of that family will be declared the so-called *winner*. The first phase of the lottery has been completed, establishing that Bill Hutchinson holds the *winning* ticket, although not quite the end game. Bill now has to formally name the five members of his household, himself included, whose names will be added to the black box for the final drawing.

Tessie Hutchinson voices her dissatisfaction and anger.

People began to look around to see the Hutchinsons. Bill Hutchinson was standing quiet, staring down at the paper in his hand. Suddenly, Tessie Hutchinson shouted to Mr. Summers. "You didn't give him time enough to take any paper he wanted. I saw you. It wasn't fair!"

"Be a good sport, Tessie," Mrs. Delacroix called, and Mrs. Graves said, "All of us took the same chance."

"Shut up, Tessie," Bill Hutchinson said.

When asked by Joe Summers, as a matter of formality, if Bill had any other household members in his family, Tessie yells, "There's Don and Eva. Make *them* take their chance!" referring to her married daughter Eva and son-in-law Don (both non-household members). This is certainly an extreme example of **dramatic irony** because Tessie is grasping at straws; surely someone in the Hutchinson household is certain to die that morning. Mr. Summers is quick to point out that daughters draw with their husbands' families. "You know that as well as anyone else," he delicately puts to Tessie.

This is the **turning point** in the story, for it is now *clearly* evident that *winning* the lottery is a *losing* proposition. Although you had the distinct advantage of knowing the negative outcome by having read the last few sentences earlier, we, nonetheless, were given many hints throughout the narrative via **literary symbols** and **dramatic irony**. The *average* reader (if I may be permitted to define the term loosely) might not have had a clue as to what is really going on concerning *The Lottery* if one is not in tune with the elements that prefigure this classic short story—at least not until the **turning point** in the narrative.

Five slips of paper with the Hutchinson family member names have been added to the black box by Mr. Graves. The slips include the names of Bill's three children (Bill Jr., Nancy, and little Dave), his wife Tessie, and himself. Each household member will now come forward and select a slip of paper. One of the slips reveals the dreaded circular coal-mark, dramatically determining the *winner*—who will lose his or her life.

"It wasn't fair," Tessie repeated. "I think we ought to start over," she says quietly. "I tell you it wasn't *fair*. You didn't give him time enough to choose. Everybody saw that."

As Mr. Graves added those five slips to the box, he intentionally drops the remaining slips of paper on the ground as part of the ritual, "where the breeze caught them and lifted them off." Here is an example of multi-level **literary symbolism**, for those many slips of paper not only symbolize the villagers' *ephemeral existence*, the *frailty of human life*, but also serve as a **symbol** for seeds, seeds that fall upon a barren, rocky ground (the village square), which *curtails growth*.

Keep the image of barrenness alive in your mind for a moment, and think back to the beginning of the story when you are first introduced to Mr. Summers.

"He was a round-faced, jovial man and he ran the coal business, and people were sorry for him, because he had no children and his wife was a scold."

This suggests a sterile condition in which no life thrives.

The subtle **symbol** of barrenness in the beginning of the story ties in quite neatly with the more salient symbol of *effeteness* (lacking the power to bear offspring or produce fruit in this sense), representative of that barren plot where Mr. Summers, the director of death, conducts the lottery each year. What better business operation could Shirley Jackson have assigned one of her main characters than the coal company business? Perhaps a funeral director? As coal is *mined underground*, how befitting that the author applies a dark underworld connection, creating an existential microcosm, a community embodied in a circle of *evil*, their rural world caught up in chaos and confusion—a world without God.

One at a time, the five members of the Hutchinson household come forward to draw a slip from the box, being reminded to keep their paper folded until each person has drawn. Little Dave went first, and Mr. Graves helped the boy. Twelve-year-old Nancy is next, followed by Bill Jr. Behind her eldest son goes Tessie, quite defiantly, snatching the folded slip from the box. Finally, Bill Hutchinson steps forth anew, withdrawing the last slip of paper from the box.

The folded slips of paper are about to be opened. Again, Mr. Graves helps little Dave by unfolding the boy's paper. The slip is blank, and a sigh of relief is issued from the crowd, for had the young boy drawn the winning ticket, he was sure to be stoned by the villagers. Nancy and Bill Jr. opened theirs. The slips are blank; both brother and sister beam and laugh, raising their hands above their heads to show the crowd. The great **irony** is, of course, that their sudden relief must eventually be mixed with horrendous emotions concerning their parents, for the winner of the lottery has now been narrowed down to either Bill Hutchinson or his wife, Tessie. One of them will be sacrificed (murdered). To create even greater suspense, the author has Mr. Summers address Tessie to show her slip of paper. Tessie hesitates. Mr. Summers has Bill Hutchinson show his own paper; it is blank. That leaves Tessie. This becomes the moment of truth, the final resolution referred to as **dénouement**—the unraveling of the complexities of a **plot** (story development).

"It's Tessie," Mr. Summers said, and his voice was hushed. "Show us her paper, Bill."
Bill Hutchinson went over to his wife and forced the slip of paper out of her hand. It had a black spot on it, the black spot Mr. Summers had made the night before with the heavy pencil in the coal company office. Bill Hutchinson held it up, and there was a stir in the crowd.

The black spot is yet another **symbol** signifying a circle; a circle of evil surrounding a community of villagers. There is great **irony** that follows with Mr. Summers' announcement:

"All right, folks," Mr. Summers said, "let's finish quickly."

Yes, indeed. Let's finish quickly so that we can get back before noontime, have our lunch, and go on about our business as though nothing out of the ordinary has happened that morning; that is, until next year when the villagers will continue their annual tradition is what Shirley Jackson is telling us through her use of **dramatic irony**.
And so, the villagers move toward the pile of stones that the boys had readied earlier, unobtrusively slipped in at the beginning of the story under the guise of 'boys will be boys,' noting nothing unusual about such behavior. Now, however, the author's insertion and message become quite clear. The stones are to be used as a ritual stoning, a sacrificial offering to ensure a good crop year. It is a stone's throw (pun intended) from an annual quasi form of entertainment enjoyed by folks like Old Man Warner and the director of death, himself, Joe Summers. The event is supplemented by such civic activities as the village square dances, the teenage club, and the Halloween program—inevitably followed by a 'day of death' relished, too, by a sadistic few who lead the pack like wild dogs:

The pile of stones the boys had made earlier was ready; there were stones on the ground with the blowing scraps of paper that had come out of the box. Mrs. Delacroix selected a stone so large she had to pick it up with both hands and turned to Mrs. Dunbar. "Come on," she said. "Hurry up."
Mrs. Dunbar had small stones in both hands, and she said, gasping for breath. "I can't run at all. You'll have to go ahead and I'll catch up with you."

The children had stones already. And someone gave little Davy Hutchinson a few pebbles.

Certainly, the great **irony** here is that one sadistic soul gives little Davy Hutchinson some pebbles to contribute to the stoning of his own mother. Tessie is in the very center of that cleared, barren space. A stone has already hit her in the head. Old Man Warner is encouraging the crowd to advance. Adams (our first man) leads the pack with Mrs. Graves right beside him.

"It isn't fair, it isn't right," Mrs. Hutchinson screamed, and then they were upon her.

The ability to identify literary symbols and recognize dramatic irony requires perception. The capacity to skillfully employ these elements demands a labor of love. As discussed earlier, symbolism and irony serve to create compactness, which the literary storywriter endeavors to attain. The following is a list of the literary symbols we've covered in *The Lottery*.

pile of stones = ritual stoning (Biblical overtone)
dust = death and/or decay
cross = symbol of Christianity (in this case, perverted)
black wooden box = mini-coffin
slips of paper = seeds; personify villagers' ephemeral existence; frailty of human life
village square = barren, rocky ground; growth impossible; sterile condition
coal = black (portent of disaster, wickedness, evil); mined underground; dark underworld connection = devilish doings
black spot = circle of evil

Adams = first man: natural tendency towards sin (Biblical overtone); first to draw in the lottery; foremost in the crowd of villagers, leading the pack like wild dogs.

Delacroix = cross; "Mrs. Delacroix selected a stone so large she had to pick it up with both hands," with which to smash Tessie Hutchinson.

Graves = place of burial; Mrs. Graves right alongside Mr. Adams, about to stone Tessie Hutchinson.

Warner = forewarning; Warner = mini-war being waged.

You had a choice of continuing with this lesson or pausing to first read the story then returning to the lesson and discussion. In either case, your antenna is now up and fine-tuned. The following is *The Lottery* in its entirety. Enjoy the wide world of literature.

The Lottery
by Shirley Jackson

The morning of June 27th was clear and sunny, with the fresh warmth of a full-summer day; the flowers were blossoming profusely and the grass was richly green. The people of the village began to gather in the square, between the post office and the bank, around ten o'clock; in some towns there were so many people that the lottery took two days and had to be started on June 26th, but in this village, where there were only about three hundred people, the whole lottery took less than two hours, so it could begin at ten o'clock in the morning and still be through in time to allow the villagers to get home for noon dinner.

The children assembled first, of course. School was recently over for the summer, and the feeling of liberty sat uneasily on most of them; they tended to gather together quietly for a while before they broke into boisterous play, and their talk was still of the classroom and the teacher, of books and reprimands. Bobby Martin had already stuffed his pockets full of stones, and the other boys soon followed his example, selecting the smoothest and roundest stones; Bobby and Harry Jones and Dickie Delacroix—the villagers pronounced this name "Dellacroy"—eventually made a great pile of stones in one corner of the square and guarded it against the raids of the other boys. The girls stood aside, talking among themselves, looking over their shoulders at the boys, and the very small children rolled in the dust or clung to the hands of their older brothers or sisters.

Soon the men began to gather, surveying their own children, speaking of planting and rain, tractors and taxes. They stood together, away from the pile of stones in the corner, and their jokes were quiet and they smiled rather than laughed. The women, wearing faded house dresses and sweaters, came shortly after their menfolk. They greeted one another and exchanged bits of gossip as they went to join their husbands. Soon the women, standing by their husbands, began to call to their children, and the children came reluctantly, having to be called four or five times. Bobby Martin ducked under his mother's grasping hand and ran, laughing, back to the pile of stones. His father spoke up sharply, and Bobby came quickly and took his place between his father and his oldest brother.

The lottery was conducted—as were the square dances, the teenage club, the Halloween program—by Mr. Summers, who had time and energy to devote to civic activities. He was a round-faced, jovial man and he ran the coal business, and people were sorry for him, because he had no children and his wife was a scold. When he arrived in the square, carrying the black wooden box, there was a murmur of conversation among the villagers, and he waved and called, "Little late today, folks." The postmaster, Mr. Graves, followed him, carrying a three-legged stool, and the stool was put in the center of the square and Mr. Summers set the black box down on it. The villagers kept their distance, leaving a space between themselves and the stool, and when Mr. Summers said, "Some of you fellows want to give me a hand?" there was a hesitation before two men, Mr. Martin and his oldest son, Baxter, came forward to hold the box steady on the stool while Mr. Summers stirred up the papers inside it.

The original paraphernalia for the lottery had been lost long ago, and the black box now resting on the stool had been put into use even before Old Man Warner, the oldest man in town, was born. Mr. Summers spoke frequently to the villagers about making a new box, but no one liked to upset even as much tradition as was represented by the black box. There was a story that the present box had been made with some pieces of the box that had preceded it, the one that had been constructed when the first people settled down to make a village here. Every year, after the lottery, Mr. Summers began talking again about a new box, but every year the subject was allowed to fade off without anything's being done. The black box grew shabbier each year; by now it was no longer completely black but splintered badly along one side to show the original wood color, and in some places faded or stained.

Mr. Martin and his oldest son, Baxter, held the black box securely on the stool until Mr. Summers had stirred the papers thoroughly with his hand. Because so much of the ritual had been forgotten or discarded, Mr. Summers had been successful in having slips of paper substituted for the chips of wood that had been used for generations. Chips of wood, Mr. Summers had argued, had been all very well when the village was tiny, but now that the population was more than three hundred and likely to keep on growing, it was necessary to use something that would fit more easily into the black box. The night before the lottery, Mr. Summers and Mr. Graves made up the slips of paper and put them in the box, and it was then taken to the safe of Mr. Summers's coal company and locked up until Mr. Summers was ready to take it to the square next morning. The rest of the year, the box was put way, sometimes one place, sometimes another; it had spent one year in Mr. Graves's barn and another year underfoot in the post office, and sometimes it was set on a shelf in the Martin grocery and left there.

There was a great deal of fussing to be done before Mr. Summers declared the lottery open. There were the lists to make up—of heads of families, heads of households in each family, members of each household in each family. There was the proper swearing-in of Mr. Summers by the postmaster, as the official of the lottery; at one time, some people remembered, there had been a recital of some sort, performed by the official of the lottery, a perfunctory, tuneless chant that had been rattled off duly each year; some people believed that the official of the lottery used to stand just so when he said or sang it, others believed that he was supposed to walk among the people, but years and years ago this part of the ritual had been allowed to lapse. There had been, also, a ritual salute, which the official of the lottery had had to use in addressing each person who came up to draw from the box, but this also had changed with time, until now it was felt necessary only for the official to speak to each person approaching. Mr. Summers was very good at all this; in his clean white shirt and blue jeans, with one hand resting carelessly on the black box, he seemed very proper and important as he talked interminably to Mr. Graves and the Martins.

Just as Mr. Summers finally left off talking and turned to the assembled villagers, Mrs. Hutchinson came hurriedly along the path to the square, her sweater thrown over her shoulders, and slid into place in the back of the crowd. "Clean forgot what day it was," she said to Mrs. Delacroix, who stood next to her, and they both laughed softly. "Thought my old man was out back stacking wood," Mrs. Hutchinson went on, "and then I looked out the window and the kids were gone, and then I remembered it was the twenty-seventh and came a-running." She dried her hands on her apron, and Mrs. Delacroix said, "You're in time, though. They're still talking away up there."

Mrs. Hutchinson craned her neck to see through the crowd and found her husband and children standing near the front. She tapped Mrs. Delacroix on the arm as a farewell and began to make her way through the crowd. The people separated good-humoredly to let her through: two or three people said, in voices just loud enough to be heard across the crowd, "Here comes your Missus, Hutchinson," and "Bill, she made it after all." Mrs. Hutchinson reached her husband, and Mr. Summers, who had been waiting, said cheerfully, "Thought we were going to have to get on without you, Tessie." Mrs. Hutchinson said, grinning, "Wouldn't have me leave m'dishes in the sink, now would you, Joe?" and soft laughter ran through the crowd as the people stirred back into position after Mrs. Hutchinson's arrival.

"Well, now," Mr. Summers said soberly, "guess we better get started, get this over with, so's we can go back to work. Anybody ain't here?"

"Dunbar," several people said. "Dunbar, Dunbar."

Mr. Summers consulted his list. "Clyde Dunbar," he said. "That's right. He's broke his leg, hasn't he? Who's drawing for him?"

"Me, I guess," a woman said, and Mr. Summers turned to look at her. "Wife draws for her husband," Mr. Summers said. "Don't you have a grown boy to do it for you, Janey?" Although Mr. Summers and everyone else in the village knew the answer perfectly well, it was the business of the official of the lottery to ask such questions formally. Mr. Summers waited with an expression of polite interest while Mrs. Dunbar answered.

"Horace's not but sixteen yet," Mrs. Dunbar said regretfully. "Guess I gotta fill in for the old man this year."

"Right," Mr. Summers said. He made a note on the list he was holding. Then he asked, "Watson boy drawing this year?"

A tall boy in the crowd raised his hand. "Here," he said. "I'm drawing for m'mother and me." He blinked his eyes nervously and ducked his head as several voices in the crowd said things like, "Good fellow, Jack," and "Glad to see your mother's got a man to do it."

"Well," Mr. Summers said, "guess that's everyone. Old Man Warner make it?"

"Here," a voice said, and Mr. Summers nodded.

A sudden hush fell on the crowd as Mr. Summers cleared his throat and looked at the list. "All ready?" he called. "Now, I'll read the names—heads of families first—and the men come up and take a paper out of the box. Keep the paper folded in your hand without looking at it until everyone has had a turn. Everything clear?"

The people had done it so many times that they only half listened to the directions: most of them were quiet, wetting their lips, not looking around. Then Mr.

Summers raised one hand high and said, "Adams." A man disengaged himself from the crowd and came forward. "Hi, Steve," Mr. Summers said, and Mr. Adams said, "Hi, Joe." They grinned at one another humorlessly and nervously. Then Mr. Adams reached into the black box and took out a folded paper. He held it firmly by one corner as he turned and went hastily back to his place in the crowd, where he stood a little apart from his family, not looking down at his hand.

"Allen," Mr. Summers said. "Anderson.... Bentham."

"Seems like there's no time at all between lotteries any more," Mrs. Delacroix said to Mrs. Graves in the back row. "Seems like we got through with the last one only last week."

"Time sure goes fast," Mrs. Graves said.

"Clark.... Delacroix."

"There goes my old man," Mrs. Delacroix said. She held her breath while her husband went forward.

"Dunbar," Mr. Summers said, and Mrs. Dunbar went steadily to the box while one of the women said, "Go on, Janey," and another said, "There she goes."

"We're next," Mrs. Graves said. She watched while Mr. Graves came around from the side of the box, greeted Mr. Summers gravely, and selected a slip of paper from the box. By now, all through the crowd there were men holding the small folded papers in their large hands, turning them over and over nervously. Mrs. Dunbar and her two sons stood together, Mrs. Dunbar holding the slip of paper.

"Harburt.... Hutchinson."

"Get up there, Bill," Mrs. Hutchinson said, and the people near her laughed.

"Jones."

"They do say," Mr. Adams said to Old Man Warner, who stood next to him, "that over in the north village they're talking of giving up the lottery."

Old Man Warner snorted. "Pack of crazy fools," he said. "Listening to the young folks, nothing's good enough for *them*. Next thing you know, they'll be wanting to go back to living in caves, nobody work any more, live *that* way for a while. Used to be a saying about 'Lottery in June, corn be heavy soon.' First thing you know, we'd all be eating stewed chickweed and acorns. There's *always* been a lottery," he added petulantly. "Bad enough to see young Joe Summers up there joking with everybody."

"Some places have already quit lotteries," Mrs. Adams said.

"Nothing but trouble in *that*," Old Man Warner said stoutly. "Pack of young fools."

"Martin." And Bobby Martin watched his father go forward. "Overdyke.... Percy."

"I wish they'd hurry," Mrs. Dunbar said to her older son. "I wish they'd hurry."

"They're almost through," her son said.

"You get ready to run tell Dad," Mrs. Dunbar said.

Mr. Summers called his own name and then stepped forward precisely and selected a slip from the box. Then he called, "Warner."

"Seventy-seventh year I been in the lottery," Old Man Warner said as he went through the crowd. "Seventy-seventh time."

"Watson." The tall boy came awkwardly through the crowd. Someone said, "Don't be nervous, Jack," and Mr. Summers said, "Take your time, son."

"Zanini."

After that, there was a long pause, a breathless pause, until Mr. Summers, holding his slip of paper in the air, said, "All right, fellows." For a minute, no one moved, and then all the slips of paper were opened. Suddenly, all the women began to speak at once, saying, "Who is it?" "Who's got it?" "Is it the Dunbars?" "Is it the Watsons?" Then the voices began to say, "It's Hutchinson. It's Bill." "Bill Hutchinson's got it."

"Go tell your father," Mrs. Dunbar said to her older son.

People began to look around to see the Hutchinsons. Bill Hutchinson was standing quiet, staring down at the paper in his hand. Suddenly, Tessie Hutchinson shouted to Mr. Summers. "You didn't give him time enough to take any paper he wanted. I saw you. It wasn't fair!"

"Be a good sport, Tessie," Mrs. Delacroix called, and Mrs. Graves said, "All of us took the same chance."

"Shut up, Tessie," Bill Hutchinson said.

"Well, everyone," Mr. Summers said, "that was done pretty fast, and now we've got to be hurrying a little more to get done in time." He consulted his next list. "Bill," he said, "you draw for the Hutchinson family. You got any other households in the Hutchinsons?"

"There's Don and Eva," Mrs. Hutchinson yelled. "Make *them* take their chance!"

"Daughters draw with their husbands' families, Tessie," Mr. Summers said gently. "You know that as well as anyone else."

"It wasn't fair," Tessie said.

"I guess not, Joe." Bill Hutchinson said regretfully. "My daughter draws with her husband's family; that's only fair. And I've got no other family except the kids."

"Then, as far as drawing for families is concerned, it's you," Mr. Summers said in explanation, "and as far as drawing for households is concerned, that's you, too. Right?"

"Right," Bill Hutchinson said.

"How many kids, Bill?" Mr. Summers asked formally.

"Three," Bill Hutchinson said. "There's Bill, Jr., and Nancy, and little Dave. And Tessie and me."

"All right, then," Mr. Summers said. "Harry, you got their tickets back?"

Mr. Graves nodded and held up the slips of paper. "Put them in the box, then," Mr. Summers directed. "Take Bill's and put it in."

"I think we ought to start over," Mrs. Hutchinson said, as quietly as she could. "I tell you it wasn't *fair*. You didn't give him time enough to choose. *Every*body saw that."

Mr. Graves had selected the five slips and put them in the box, and he dropped all the papers but those onto the ground, where the breeze caught them and lifted them off.

"Listen, everybody," Mrs. Hutchinson was saying to the people around her.

"Ready, Bill?" Mr. Summers asked, and Bill Hutchinson, with one quick glance around at his wife and children nodded.

"Remember," Mr. Summers said, "take the slips and keep them folded until each person has taken one. Harry, you help little Dave." Mr. Graves took the hand of the little boy, who came willingly with him up to the box. "Take a paper out of the box, Davy," Mr. Summers said. Davy put his hand into the box and laughed. "Take just *one* paper," Mr. Summers said. "Harry, you hold it for him." Mr. Graves took the child's hand and removed the folded paper from the tight fist and held it while little Dave stood next to him and looked up at him wonderingly.

"Nancy next," Mr. Summers said. Nancy was twelve, and her school friends breathed heavily as she went forward, switching her skirt, and took a slip daintily from the box. "Bill, Jr.," Mr. Summers said, and Billy, his face red and his feet overlarge, nearly knocked the box over as he got a paper out. "Tessie," Mr. Summers said. She hesitated for a minute, looking around defiantly, and then set her lips and went up to the box. She snatched a paper out and held it behind her.

"Bill," Mr. Summers said, and Bill Hutchinson reached into the box and felt around, bringing his hand out at last with the slip of paper in it.

The crowd was quiet. A girl whispered, "I hope it's not Nancy," and the sound of the whisper reached the edges of the crowd.

"It's not the way it used to be," Old Man Warner said clearly. "People ain't the way they used to be."

"All right," Mr. Summers said. "Open the papers. Harry, you open little Dave's."

Mr. Graves opened the slip of paper and there was a general sigh through the crowd as he held it up and everyone could see that it was blank. Nancy and Bill, Jr. opened theirs at the same time, and both beamed and laughed, turning around to the crowd and holding their slips of paper above their heads.

"Tessie," Mr. Summers said. There was a pause, and then Mr. Summers looked at Bill Hutchinson, and Bill unfolded his paper and showed it. It was blank.

"It's Tessie," Mr. Summers said, and his voice was hushed. "Show us her paper, Bill."

Bill Hutchinson went over to his wife and forced the slip of paper out of her hand. It had a black spot on it, the black spot Mr. Summers had made the night before with the heavy pencil in the coal-company office. Bill Hutchinson held it up, and there was a stir in the crowd.

"All right, folks," Mr. Summers said, "let's finish quickly."

Although the villagers had forgotten the ritual and lost the original black box, they still remembered to use stones. The pile of stones the boys had made earlier was ready; there were stones on the ground with the blowing scraps of paper that had come out of the box. Mrs. Delacroix selected a stone so large she had to pick it up with both hands and turned to Mrs. Dunbar. "Come on," she said. "Hurry up."

Mrs. Dunbar had small stones in both hands, and she said, gasping for breath, "I can't run at all. You'll have to go ahead and I'll catch up with you."

The children had stones already. And someone gave little Davy Hutchinson a few pebbles.

Tessie Hutchinson was in the center of a cleared space by now, and she held her hands out desperately as the villagers moved in on her. "It isn't fair," she said. A stone hit her on the side of the head.

Old Man Warner was saying, "Come on, come on, everyone." Steve Adams was in the front of the crowd of villagers, with Mrs. Graves beside him.

"It isn't fair, it isn't right," Mrs. Hutchinson screamed, and then they were upon her.

LESSON 4

WRITING WELL:
DEVELOPMENT OF A SINGLE SENTENCE
Saying What You Mean

Let us take a single thought, the seed of a sentence, shaping and formulating it into clear, concise language and imagery. Perhaps the sentence could serve as an introduction to one character, possibly two. Let's rework the sentence better than a dozen times to make it *sing*. Although this is not primarily a basic skills course, I will work in an important grammar lesson that needs to be addressed. Also, we will reinforce some of our earlier lessons concerning a 'treasure trove of tools,' adding new ones to the collection. Here we go:

Charlie was Karen's hero.

Ask yourself why? Why was Charlie Karen's hero? Now, hold that thought and let's continue building the sentence.

Charlie was Karen's hero, raising chickens for feathers.

Stop and ask yourself who is raising chickens for feathers? Charlie or Karen?
In the phrase Charlie was Karen's hero, raising chickens for feathers, Karen has been placed nearer to the phrase raising chickens for their feathers than Charlie. Therefore, it seems as though Karen raises chickens for feathers, not Charlie. But that's not what I mean to say. Nor do I mean to imply that those feathers are somehow shared between Charlie and Karen. I want Charlie as the character who raises chickens for their feathers. The first of these often repeated grammar errors is referred to as a misplaced modifier. In this case, the misplaced modifier is simply the intended name that is not placed near enough to the phrase it is supposed to modify in order to make clear that it is Charlie who is raising chickens for feathers, thereby resulting in confusion. Let's immediately clean up these types of problems by thinking carefully and rearranging words and/or adding and subtracting other words in order to have the sentence say what I mean it to say.

Karen worshiped Charlie as her hero, raising chickens for feathers, not food.

Perhaps I've now eliminated the ambiguity, or can their identities be made even clearer? In a moment we'll see, but for now it's fairly clear that Charlie is the one who raises chickens for feathers.

I have Charlie raising chickens and have decided on having Karen working in a slaughterhouse. Hence, I'll create a curious **juxtaposition** between my two characters: a slaughterhouse referencing the processing of food for consumer consumption, contrasting a kind of farm where chickens are raised for their feathers, not food. Let's build upon that imagery by employing **alliteration**. Remember? Alliteration is stressed initial sounds.

In a world where Karen saw death every day . . .

Let's change the words *every day* and give the phrase some balance with w's and d's.

In a world where Karen saw death daily . . .

Here, we've used two pairs of consonant sounds, w's and d's, for emphasis: *world where* and *death daily*.

In a world where Karen saw death daily, she worshiped Charlie as her hero, raising chickens for feathers, not food.

Note the position of the pronoun [she] and the noun [feathers], the latter of which belongs to those of the birds; therefore, let's make that image perfectly clear.

In a world where Karen saw death daily, she worshiped Charlie as her hero, raising chickens for the birds' feathers, not food. The apostrophe after the word birds' shows the plural possessive case; that is, the feathers belonging to more than just one bird. If we were talking about the feathers belonging to a single bird, which we're not, it would be written as the bird's feathers. I just snuck in another grammar point, sneaky fellow that I am.

Next, I've suddenly decided on a name change because in my mind's eye, the character's new name will later serve as a significant metaphor: Thus, I've switched Karen to Heather:

In a world where Heather saw death daily, she worshiped Charlie as her hero, raising chickens for the birds' feathers, not food.

Charlie works as a sort of grower who raises birds, as one might grow pretty flowers. Let's smooth out the **syntax** (meaning, the way we string our words together) in order to clean up any ambiguity that might still exist.

In a world where Heather saw death daily, she worshiped Charlie as her hero, watching him raise his chickens for the birds' feathers, not food.

Heather watching him makes the image clearer. The pronouns him and his help clear up any possible confusion.
Let's tack on a **simile** in order to expand the imagery.

In a world where Heather saw death daily, she worshiped Charlie as her hero, watching him raise his chickens for the birds' feathers, not food—like a grower who raises pretty flowers.

Concerning Charlie, let's paint an even clearer picture of the man in the mind of the reader.

In a world where Heather saw death daily, she worshiped Charlie as her hero, watching the old man raise his chickens for the birds' feathers, not food—like a grower who raises pretty flowers.

Let's do the same for Heather.

In a world where the attractive teenager saw death daily, Heather worshiped Charlie as her hero, watching the old man raise his chickens for the birds' feathers, not food—like a grower who raises pretty flowers.

Repetitive words (and forms thereof) within a sentence, a paragraph, or even throughout a chapter, tend to weaken writing. Note raise and raises found within this single sentence:

In a world where the attractive teenager saw death daily, Heather worshiped Charlie as her hero, watching the old man raise his chickens for their feathers, not food—like a grower who raises pretty flowers.

Let's select a better word choice referencing the second instance; that is, the word raises.

In a world where the attractive teenager saw death daily, Heather worshiped Charlie as her hero, watching the old man raise his chickens for their feathers, not food—like a grower who cultivates pretty flowers.

Cultivates is a far better word choice in that the verb means to foster growth; too, it pulls us away from repetitiveness.

In a world where the attractive teenager saw death daily, Heather worshiped Charlie as her hero, watching the old man raise his chickens for the birds' feathers, not food—like a grower who cultivates pretty flowers.

Now, let's *see* those feathers; we need a descriptive adjective:

In a world where the attractive teenager saw death daily, Heather worshiped Charlie as her hero, watching the old man raise his chickens for their vibrant colored feathers, not food—like a grower who cultivates pretty flowers.

Although descriptive, vibrant colored feathers is somewhat forced here and not entirely accurate because the feathers are generally *dun* colored; that is, a brownish-gray—a rather dull, subtle, natural color depicting, in part, aquatic life that flytiers wish to mimic for anglers. The product that feather farms are primarily concerned with must meet specific color, shape, and size requirements, at which point the feathers are graded for their quality. Again, brownish-gray is hardly a vibrant color. Hence, the word *pretty*, for pretty flowers, does not work either. What to do? Now that you're aware of this dilemma, let's look for better word choices, reworking the sentence to say what we want it to mean.

In a world where the attractive teenager saw death daily, Heather worshiped Charlie as her hero, watching the old man raise his chickens for the birds' exotic feathers, not food—like a grower who cultivates unusual flowers.

Had I not done extensive research concerning 'hackle feather farms,' which is anything but a cottage industry but rather a lucrative business that sells to fly-fishing shops, professional flytiers, as well as fly fishermen around the globe, I might not have realized this. The point is that you have to know what you're writing about. Write what you truly understand, and if you don't *know*, research the hell out of it until you do. Part of your job is to build **verisimilitude** (credibility) into your work.

Well, we're finally there, having *cultivated* a single seed of thought: Charlie was Karen's hero . . . into a full-grown (pun intended) sentence:

In a world where the attractive teenager saw death daily, Heather worshiped Charlie as her hero, watching the old man raise his chickens for the birds' exotic feathers, not food—like a grower who cultivates unusual flowers.

Later, concerning my female character's eating habits, I'll probably paint Heather as a vegetarian. Are you beginning to get the picture of the work that goes into carefully crafted writing? Of course, not every sentence has to be labored over as we have done here . . . just those where it is important to paint a very clear picture of what you are trying to convey.

If you have absorbed these lessons thus far, you are on your way to writing well. This is not to say that some of you haven't already arrived.

Just for giggles—not necessarily to tickle your fancy—check out Whiting Farms, Inc., or Metz Feathers on the Internet. You'll be educated and entertained. Good writing incorporates continued research. You never stop learning.

****

The Oxford (or serial) Comma

As I have already drawn from my knowledge of feathers for fly-tying materials, allow me to sneak in another important grammar point. What I am constantly asked in classes and writing groups is the placement of a comma before the end of a list of items. Presented as an example taken from my fishing handbook titled *The Fishing Smart Anywhere Handbook ~ For Salt Water and Fresh Water,* it includes a section on fly tying. Because there are a zillion colors and shades referencing feathers and threads with which to tie flies, I instruct readers as to some of the basic colors that they'll need to get started:

Correct: For starting out, I'll suggest ordering colors of feathers and threads that will cover a variety of patterns: gray, brown, olive, black, red, and white.

If I were to remove the last comma in the sentence above, technically, readers would be ordering a combination of red *and* white feathers and mixed color threads. That's not what I mean; therefore, the comma is needed to separate red, and white. Common sense should dictate, not a single hard-and-fast rule, which is rather silly in itself.

Incorrect: For starting out, I'll suggest ordering colors of feathers and threads that will cover a variety of patterns: gray, brown, olive, black, red and white.

Let's belabor the point in order to reinforce it.

On Sunday mornings, I enjoy juice, English muffin, eggs and coffee.

In the sentence above, those eggs are somehow mixed in with the coffee; therefore, it would be better to separate the eggs from the coffee with a comma as shown:

On Sunday mornings, I enjoy juice, English muffin, eggs, and coffee.

Let's expand on this by adding another element, bacon:

On Sunday mornings, I enjoy juice, English muffin, bacon and eggs, and coffee.

Because bacon and eggs go together like a hand and glove, it is perfectly all right to connect bacon and eggs *without* the separation of a comma, then tacking on, and coffee as seen in the previous example.

Also, we could reconstruct the sentence to read as such:

On Sunday mornings, I enjoy juice, English muffin, coffee, bacon and eggs.

I like the formation of the following sentence best because its arrangement is set in the order in which *I* enjoy my breakfast:

On Sunday mornings, I enjoy juice, English muffin, bacon and eggs, and coffee.

Some style guides and grammar books insist on the Oxford comma; others do not, such as The Associated Press (AP) Stylebook, the journalist's bible. Again, let common sense and preference prevail.

****

Let's take another look at that multisyllabic word, **verisimilitude**; that is, the building of realism or its appearance into your writings. If your story lacks credibility, the work is doomed from the start. Allow me to give you an example of how I go about building believability into my award-winning novels and current manuscripts.

As most of my fiction writing relates to serial killers, I make it my business to learn everything that I can about them. Admittedly, referencing my first novel, *Dicky, Richard, and I* (originally published as *No Stranger Than I*), I relied heavily on readings and what I had seen on TV. After all, I did not know any multiple murderers. What else was I to do? Well, along came the first death penalty case on Long Island in practically a quarter of a century at the time, that being, the Robert Shulman serial killer trial in my hometown of Riverhead, Long Island, New York. I had attended the trial as a spectator for a fifteen-month period, sitting through pretrial, trial, and the penalty phase of this case. Robert Shulman had been sentenced to death—although it wouldn't come to pass. However, that was hardly the point. What had been absolutely significant was that I had made it my business to speak with virtually every player involved in the Shulman matter; that is, the lawyers for the defense and prosecution, homicide detectives, including Lieutenant Detective John Gierasch, then the commanding officer of the Suffolk County Homicide Squad, forensic scientists, the Capital Defender's Office, correction facility officials, psychiatrists, psychologists, *Newsday*, and *New York Law Journal* reporters, Channels 11 and 12 reporters, the Long Island/Metro area chapter of Parents of Murdered Children, chief of appeals bureau members, jurors, and alternates. I had an article published regarding the Shulman case in *The Southampton Press*. Most importantly, I had thoroughly studied the defendant and the case for well over a year.

As a result of my having attended the Robert Shulman serial killer trial, I was invited to lecture before students and psychiatrists at Kirby Forensic Psychiatric Center on Ward's Island, just east of Manhattan. Thus, I was able to build a greater degree of credibility into my writings. I appeared on Enzo and Jeanine Magnozzi's two Cablevision programs: *Literally Speaking* and *Off The Cuff*. Additionally, I had given both formal and informal talks at libraries and other venues where I discussed the serial killer phenomenon, FBI profiling, as well as the writing process. Eventually, I was given my own Cablevision show, *Special Interests with Bob and Donna* (my partner of forty-five years).

Having visited and lectured at Kirby was an invaluable experience, for I was given an extensive tour of the center's maximum security mental hospital—both the men's and women's facilities—having met and spoken with some of the institution's worst offenders. I stood in the midst of their veritable environment. I had seen an actual crash room, otherwise known as the padded cell or so-caller rubber room. I had sat in the director's office, speaking at length with Dr. Bruce H. David while taking in my entire surroundings.

Consequently, when I had set the scene for one of my novels in progress, the sense of **spatial description** when describing Kirby's grounds, its buildings, the patients' areas, and the psychiatrist's office, coupled to the essence of a torrential rainy morning (which, indeed, it was), the staging squarely remains a faithful portrayal. Here is an example of that realism, excerpted from an early chapter of my award-winning novel titled *The Teacher*:

The Teacher
Chapter Two [excerpt]

Without letup, a heavy afternoon March wind whipped the southwest wall of Kirby Forensic Psychiatric Center on Ward's Island, situated on the East River, two-thirds of a mile east of Manhattan. A sudden downpour pelted, then steadily pounded the tall brick building as a gale force wind drove the gelid rain against barred or grated window panes, distorting the dismal view beyond. Within a corner office, two men sat across from one another. The hospital's director, Doctor Timothy Littleton, listened most attentively from behind his mahogany desk, staring fixedly at his straitjacketed patient.

"It's so good of you to see me, Timmy. I kept telling the others that I had precious little to say to any of them; tons of tales to tell their director." Professor Clarence Emery grinned maniacally. "Among many things, they wanted to know why I mismatched one of the heads and bodies, where I put the other, as well as why I went berserk, although I view it as nothing more than letting off a little steam. They wanted me to start at the beginning. But there is no beginning, just as surely as there is no end to it all. It's all a vicious circle. A cycle if you will, with no definitive point of reference to mark the beginning of my so-called illness."

Doctor Littleton stirred impatiently.

****

That half-day visit to Kirby led to other interesting experiences, but it all started in the courtroom when the psychiatrist for the prosecution, Dr. Bruce David, had asked me to come to the Forensic Psychiatric Center to *lecture*. He actually used the word lecture, and I almost laughed, believing that he was kidding around. When I realized that he wasn't fooling, I painstakingly explained who I was and precisely what I was doing in the courtroom. I elaborated the point that I was here to learn from such people as the good doctor.

"No, you don't understand," the director interrupted. "I've been on the stand testifying a couple of days. But you have been here from day one; you're coming to Kirby to lecture," he repeated.

And so I did, with Donna along for the ride.

Passing through a series of locked gates manned by extremely tight security very much reminded me of scenes from *The Silence of the Lambs*. The passageways were downright eerie. The sound of pelting rain hitting the building added to an all but surreal setting. I was entering the inner sanctum for the criminally insane. It was a feeling I'll never forget. I truly felt privileged for the opportunity.

Donna was not permitted to visit the maximum security section of the hospital. And although she did not receive the quintessential tour of the facilities, Donna did get to attend my lecture concerning the trial of Robert Shulman.

Considering that Shulman had been arrested by Suffolk County homicide detectives, I wanted to interview its commander, Detective Lieutenant John Gierasch, commanding officer of the homicide squad. It had taken a considerable amount of time to secure that meeting. Persistent phone calls and letters to the man eventually resulted in an interview. Though the commanding officer would not talk specifically about the Robert Shulman case, we nevertheless spoke peripherally about serial killers and other murderers. I spoke quite candidly about the plot of the novel I was writing, its characters, et cetera. I had a legal pad before me with more than two dozen questions to which I needed answers. The detective lieutenant was most generous with his information and time. I learned a great deal from the man. Like a sponge, I was absorbing my newfound knowledge and immediate surroundings. Yes, I was steadily building verisimilitude into my work. At the close of our meeting, the commanding officer told me that if I needed any further assistance, to call him. What more could I have asked for? I had made a most important contact.

There are many ways for you to go about securing essential information that will lend credibility to your writings; I have offered but a few approaches. Combined with good writing techniques, with which we'll continue, you shall significantly increase your chances of being picked up by a reputable literary agent and/or publisher.

In the following chapter, we'll take another in-depth look at avenues to explore as a wellspring of information (fodder) for your writings. It is absolutely amazing how one thing can lead to another. Take a breather before continuing. Don't rush through these chapters. Work at a pace whereby you know that you are thoroughly absorbing these valuable lessons. If need be, go back and review those sections where reinforcement may prove necessary. You are approximately a third of the way through this guidebook.

LESSON 5

THE ART OF FICTION & NONFICTION
A Mixed Bag of Tricks

In the last chapter, we covered a number of venues for collecting information that helped lend credibility to my work. I went on to explore the criminal courts concerning the Robert Shulman serial killer trial as well as two other murder cases conducted in Riverhead, N.Y.; speaking with Suffolk County homicide detectives; lecturing before students and psychiatrists at Kirby Forensic Psychiatric Center on Ward's Island; securing an interview with Detective Lieutenant John Gierasch, commander of the Suffolk County Homicide Squad; making appearances on Cablevision's *Literally Speaking* and *Off The Cuff* programs; giving informal talks and having open discussions with respect to the serial killer phenomenon, FBI profiling, as well as the writing process. All of these approaches proved invaluable. Two aspects from the above listing kept resurfacing in my mind: sanity versus insanity, coupled to death penalty legislation. Those dual elements were to become an underlying current running through my novels.

Even though the Robert Shulman serial killer trial had ended and the defendant was sentenced to death in 1999 (which never came to pass because the New York State Court of Appeals invalidated the death penalty), be reminded that the chief of homicide, Detective Lieutenant John Gierasch, would not specifically address the case with me even as late as 2001. Why? Because "It ain't over till it's over," legendary Yankee baseball player Yogi Berra, on more than one occasion, reminded us. The appeals process would run its course for approximately a decade. Going back to the time that I had spoken with homicide detectives just outside the courtroom following a short break in the Shulman proceedings, the situation remained the same. The detectives who had testified at trial referencing the killer's arrest and subsequent interrogation at police headquarters in Yaphank, N.Y., obviously, would not and could not discuss the case with me. However, as I had with their commander, we did talk *around* other cases and police procedures. The detectives proved to be a wealth of information whether conversing with me in the hallway about the weather, a cold-case file, or testifying on the stand. Spending time with their commander in his office in Yaphank was an added bonus.

Interestingly, two other death penalty cases were playing out in the Suffolk County Criminal Court building in Riverhead during the same time as the Shulman matter: People vs. Stephen LaValle, a Shirley, Long Island, N.Y. man who had been charged with the rape and murder a high-school teacher/track coach, Cynthia Quinn. I did not realize it at the time, but Cynthia Quinn was the daughter of a fellow boater whom I knew from the Moose Lodge, which is around the corner from our home in Riverhead; small world. That case resulted in a landmark decision by the New York State Court of Appeals, in which the court ruled that the state's death penalty statute was unconstitutional because of the statute's direction on how the jury was to be instructed in case of a deadlock. New York had been without the death penalty since 2004, as the law had not been amended.

Next, we have Nicholson McCoy, a powerfully built 6 foot, 5-inch tall, 275-pound man who was charged with sodomizing and killing a female co-worker at a Suffolk County grocery store in 1998. As a matter of fact, I had related some extraordinary news concerning McCoy to Detective Lieutenant Gierasch as to how the prisoner was able to open his supposedly locked cell door and move freely about the facility during late-night hours. The commander was nonplused, asking me how I knew this as well as other remarkable facts that I had communicated concerning Nicholson McCoy. The answer was that for a period of fifteen months, I had sat near or next to Andrew Smith, a consummate staff writer for *Newsday*, listening and reading every single word the man reported concerning those three death penalty cases. I had the commander's attention.

I could have made these murders into a three-ring circus, moving around from courtroom to courtroom. Although I did visit those other Parts (courtrooms) anent Stephen LaValle and Nicholson McCoy whenever there was a break re the Shulman trial, my focus was on the main attraction—Robert Shulman, serial killer! For the most part, multiple murderers are my bailiwick. Still, as a mere spectator, those brief ancillary drop-in observances to the other courtrooms later proved priceless. I had more fodder than I ever imagined.

With regard to my writing a book concerning Robert Shulman, I had discussed the idea of fiction versus nonfiction with Andrew Smith. Although the testimony we listened to was often sensational and horrific, it was not out of the ordinary. I know that might sound rather odd to some of you because of the very nature of the crimes—serial killer—multiple murderer. Yet, there was nothing really exceptional about Shulman's murders. Yes, the killings were brutal in that he lured the victims to his home and bludgeoned them to death. Yes, the victims' families suffered greatly. Yes, Robert Shulman came from a dysfunctional family. Again, there was nothing truly extraordinary about the story; that is, until I looked *beyond* the facts unfolding daily before the ears and eyes of the jury—facts concerning Robert's younger brother, Barry Shulman, who had helped dispose of the bodies. To me, that is a fascinating part of the story. Even Robert Shulman's defense attorneys thought so, for they conceived a fiction in order to create a reasonable doubt in the minds of jurors, paving the way and pointing an accusatory finger at Robert's brother, Barry, who lived directly above the defendant's apartment at 11 Glow Lane in Hicksville (Nassau County), Long Island, New York.

Robert Shulman stood as the accused serial killer, and the prosecutors kept the focus there. Both Andrew Smith and I felt that if the Shulman story were to be *told* and *sold*, it could succeed with a bit of needed embellishment. Presented as a nonfiction book, it would not necessarily seduce publishers. Presented as fiction, with the right ingredients added, it might pan out. I knew the direction that Robert Shulman's two defense attorneys were taking before they even headed there. I, too, would tell a *story*, concerning both brothers, Robert and Barry. It would become the hook in my manuscript and eventual novel titled *Trace Evidence*. Except for several courtroom scenes, the story would be loosely based on and inspired by the Robert Shulman case.

But for the moment, let's examine how I wove certain facts concerning the Nicholson McCoy case, covered earlier with Detective Lieutenant John Gierasch, Commander of Suffolk County Homicide. Detective Lieutenant John Gierasch became Detective Lieutenant Theodore Groche and is one of the main characters in my award-winning works of fiction titled *The Author*, and its sequel, *The Teacher*. Similarly, Nicholson McCoy's name has been changed to Nicholson Fitch. The characterization of Justin Barnes, my protagonist, a one-time drug dealer and gun runner, eventually working undercover for Suffolk County Homicide, figures into a four-book series—tracking down serial killers. Justin would never play a prominent role in the minds of readers had I not built absolute believability into the man and his mission.

The reinstatement of New York State's death penalty in 1995, followed by its repeal in 2004, actually as the result of the Stephen LaValle case, became of paramount importance in mounting my story and its underlying motifs. Let's take a peek. Note how I worked in my observations and experiences concerning the courts and police headquarters in Yaphank, mixing fact with fiction in my novel, *The Author*.

The Author
Chapter Fifty-Two [excerpt]

Detective Brian Archer, to whom Justin was temporarily assigned, was quite impressed at how the civilian, without the aid of any notes, could remember all the Moose Lodges in relationship to the cities and towns that so concerned the teams, having logged their respective distances to the crime scenes in preparation for York's interview with Harold Dupree.

Archer proved to be a decent sort of chap—*for a cop, that is*—the maverick entertained. A little square, but still tolerable. It was the lead detective, Dean Nelson, who fought to keep him at bay and away from the case. Ironically, Detective Andrew Miller had gone to bat for Barnes.

Of course, Justin first had to convince their lieutenant that he had information worthy of a seat and an assignment in homicide. As it turned out, it was solid intelligence that prevented a truly violent inmate from murdering someone—maybe even thwarting the career criminal's escape from Riverhead Jail. Justin simply told them how Nicholson Fitch, the third runner-up for the death penalty on Long Island, would casually walk out of his cell and quite possibly through the gate of the correctional facility itself. In any event, Fitch was sure to take a life or two in the process. That was a given, Justin knew, now that the career criminal was being held for the rape and murder of a supermarket employee.

Initially, Theo and several other detectives had a good laugh listening to the maverick's story, but afterward got on the phone with the head of security at the jail as a precautionary measure. What the corrections officers found twenty minutes later was unbelievable. Fitch had used toothpaste to glue several Scrabble tiles in the tracks of his sliding cell door, giving the appearance that it was locked when, in fact, it was merely closed. Justin knew the man and his antics well, having served time with the killer upstate years ago.

[**Note:** This is precisely how Nicholson McCoy had walked out of his cell in Riverhead Jail during evening hours, as reported [in part] in *Newsday*, May 2nd, 2000, by staff writer Andrew Smith. We'll take a look at that article later, but first we have some important ground to cover as we continue to move through the scene.]

"How in all hell did you know that?" Theo had demanded of Justin, with Nelson and Archer looking on in disbelief.

"We got a deal?" Justin asked and smiled slyly.

[**Note:** Allow me to address a very important rule concerning dialogue tags. In the above questioning (interrogative) single sentence, let's change the wording to read, "We got a deal?" Justin smiled slyly. The word smiled is not a verb of speech, and its usage is incorrect. Justin **said**, Justin **remarked**, Justin **questioned**, are, indeed, verbs of speech and is, therefore, correct. "We got a deal?" Justin smiled slyly, or Justin laughed, or Justin smirked are not verbs of speech. These types of errors make you look bad. Avoid them like the plague. Once I tacked on a verb of speech such as **asked** following the dialogue, I'm free to tag on a descriptive verb such as **smiled**. Or I could have simply left it alone: "We got a deal?" Also, I could have *begun* the sentence as follows. Justin smiled. "We got a deal?" But as long as dialogue precedes the clause, a verb of speech must follow.]

"We don't make deals with felons," Dean squawked.

[**Note:** In the above, **squawked** is certainly a verb of speech and is therefore correct.]

"Sure you do," Justin summarily corrected. "You make them all the time. They're called *flea* bargains. I scratch your back; you scratch mine. And I just scratched your fuckin' back, fellas, but mine's still itchin'," *motherfucker,* was the twelve-letter word he had in mind but held in check.

[**Note:** Justin is having a bit of fun punning on the word *flea* in lieu of *plea* bargains. Notice, too, that the profanity, *motherfucker,* is in Justin's mind, not part of the actual dialogue and is therefore italicized. Additionally, italics may be used for emphasis. Justin has a propensity for words, states, and capitals in order to educate himself, seen throughout *The Author*. An atlas and an abridged dictionary are tools that remain close at hand for a practically illiterate Justin Barnes, a man with his own brand of *justice* firmly in mind.]

"I said, we'd consider it," Theo set forth.
"Yeah? Then consider this. Fitch got himself several shivs planted in and around lockup for when he does or doesn't do his *ex·o·dus*. So, I'll jus' *think* about whether or not I'm gonna clue you in as to their whereabouts. Dig?"
The head of homicide dug, all right. Deep into Barnes' criminal record as well as Fitch's. Their past—right up to the present. There was not much of a gap between releases and resentencings for the latter. Barnes, on the other hand, had some brains and managed to sidestep the law in several instances. Fitch, sitting on the other side of the fence, was a two-time loser. The lieutenant also learned that the two did a little time together up in Attica. It was probably how Barnes knew about the Scrabble tile and toothpaste ploy, the cop figured. Theo further learned that Fitch recently stabbed an inmate in the neck with a weapon fashioned from a ballpoint pen. Another man he knifed in the shoulder—a trustee—with a blade sharpened from a spoon handle.

[**Note:** The knives referenced above are based on facts as you'll soon read for yourself in Andrew Smith's *Newsday* article.]

Seven guards had gone after him in the bathroom following that incident, and all seven took a spill when the six-foot-five fellow threw down a pail of soapy water and washed away their pride. Five wound up in the hospital from a beating. Another, crippled in a corner, wore a bucket for a helmet, while the other officer fled. Two hundred seventy-five pounds of pure muscle went after the single soul until the prisoner was finally corralled and threatened by a team of no less than thirty zookeepers brandishing batons. Fitch had calmly put up his hands and smiled knowingly:
"I surrender, man," Fitch had declared with a smirk. "But lay one o' 'dose sticks on me now, and I'll break e'ry one o' yo' punk-ass fuckin' necks later, I swear."
No one stepped within a foot of the gorilla-like monster as he coolly strode back to his cell.

[**Note:** With a bit of embellishment for dramatic effect, the event dealing with Nicholson Fitch, as a character (based on Nicholson McCoy), had actually occurred. This you will not read in Andrew Smith's *Newsday* article. I had received the information from a source well-connected with the courts and later corroborated by a corrections officer. "Nicholson McCoy is the worst we've ever seen, and I've worked here for — years," the man offered on condition of anonymity. I edited out the number of years so as not to narrow down a name. McCoy had actually thrown down that bucket of soapy water in the bathroom and fought with corrections officers.]

"All right," Theo finally said, folding uncharacteristically before the cagey felon. "You probably saved us all a headache."

"No 'bout a-doubt it," Justin swore. "Man's a mean killin' machine."

"Now, about those knives he may or may not have planted 'in and around lockup,' you said."

The deal was that Justin Barnes had to be mindful of his place, do exactly as he was told, and not question or second-guess any member on the team in exchange for the privilege of working an *important* aspect of the case. The two men shook hands. Justin was leery that the lieutenant might be giving him a snow job—maybe have him fetch coffee or doughnuts for the squad—or tell him it was *important* that the detectives all had sharpened pencils. *Some shit like that,* he figured. But Theo was true to his word. Justin Barnes was *still* working on an important facet of the case . . . following a trail that the serial killer just might be keeping to, God willing.

Amazing, dude!

Justin Barnes, cop killer as a kid, became something of a deputized assistant *hom·o·cide* detective. Monisha Washington was surely spinning in her grave.

"Doin' this for you, kid," he said to the sexy snapshot taped to the upper corner of the refrigerator. He also carried a photo of the pretty coed in his wallet. "Well, maybe a little bit for me in the bargain." He threw her a kiss as he closed the light and exited the kitchen, promising to visit her grave just as soon as this business was settled. "Bye fo' now, girl."

Justin headed for the living room then returned to the listing of Moose Lodges and his travel atlas.

****

As mentioned earlier, the Riverhead Moose Lodge is right around the corner from our home. Connected with the lodge is the Riverhead Moose Yacht Club. A wellspring of information was right at my fingertips. With respect to my protagonist, Justin Barnes, "An unlikely vigilante with a vengeance . . . " — as quoted from the back cover of *The Author* — I had discussed the story line with Detective Lieutenant John Gierasch. The plot was only in its infancy. The challenge would be to build credibility into the work. Would a reading audience buy into it? Namely, a convicted Afro-American felon working as a covert operative for Suffolk County Homicide. An uneducated man, but with the street smarts of an asphalt jungle cat, Justin Barnes is a maverick hellbent in search of Malcolm Columba—a sadistic, prolific, diabolical serial killer. Justin will hunt the man down, with or without the help of Suffolk County Homicide.

Let's now take a look at Andrew Smith's article referencing Nicholson McCoy, which appeared in *Newsday*:

Watching Defendant's Every Move / Jail Officials:

Murder suspect warrants bolstered security

Published: May 2, 2000 8:00 PM
by Andrew Smith. STAFF WRITER

Death penalty defendant Nicholson McCoy has vowed to attack fellow Suffolk County Jail inmates, correction officers and a judge and had assembled the means to carry out the threats, jail officials said yesterday.

As a result, McCoy is surrounded by court officers when he sits in a Riverhead courtroom during jury selection for his upcoming murder trial, and his legs are shackled whenever he's not in his cell, including in court.

"This guy's a problem guy," said jail Chief of Staff Alan Otto.

"If this [trial] goes bad, I'm going to kill a C.O. [correction officer]," McCoy said, according to Otto. McCoy allegedly told another officer, "I can't wait to get my hands on your little punk ---- neck."

McCoy, 38, of East Patchogue, is charged with sodomizing and stabbing to death a supermarket co-worker, Victoria Peymann, 32, of Shirley, at the Edwards Grocery in Medford in October, 1998. He faces the death penalty if convicted. Jury selection in the trial started in March and is expected to continue through next month.

Since last week, six court officers have been stationed within two steps of him while he sits in court, with two standing at arm's length behind him, staring at his every move. When he is moved in and out of the courtroom, his handcuffs are shackled to a belt cinched tight around his waist. His feet are shackled at all times, but they are hidden from jurors' view by burlap skirts on the tables in court.

The burlap was installed in March, in anticipation that it might be needed. Defense attorney Kelley Sharkey refused to comment on the extra security and its alleged cause, but she objected in March to the presence of extra court officers.

"I don't want the courtroom looking like an armed camp," she said then. "It leaves the jurors thinking Mr. McCoy is dangerous, or guilty."

Otto said McCoy's most recent problems began April 1, when he allegedly stabbed another inmate in the shoulder with a knife he had fashioned from a plastic pen. Then on April 18, Otto said a jail informant told correction officers that McCoy had another "shank," prison slang for a homemade knife. Officers searched McCoy's cell and found he had prevented his sliding cell door from closing completely by using toothpaste to glue Scrabble tiles in the tracks, Otto said. When the door was closed, it looked like it was locked, but it wasn't.

"We believe we were very fortunate," Otto said. "If he had got out at night, who knows what he could have done."

In the cell, Otto said officers found an 11½-inch shank made from the heavy-duty clothes hanger that was delivered with his court clothes. Otto said jail officials take McCoy's threats against inmates, female officers and Judge Louis Ohlig seriously. McCoy is a muscular 6 feet, 5 inches tall and weighs 275 pounds.

"He's a big guy," Otto said. "The guy's got nothing to lose."

****

If you are writing a crime novel and do not have the time to visit the courts on a daily basis as a spectator, you can certainly follow a sensational trial of this nature by picking up a newspaper, providing, of course, that the coverage is decent. In the case of Robert Shulman, et al (LaValle and McCoy), Andrew Smith's reporting was exemplary. At the conclusion of the Shulman sentencing, the presiding judge, Judge Arthur Pitts, acknowledged Mr. Smith's outstanding, accurate coverage for *Newsday*. Although *The New York Times* occasionally covered the Suffolk County Robert Shulman trial, I noted that a couple of reporters got the facts wrong. If I choose to follow a crime story occurring across the country, or any story for that matter, I would subscribe to a local newspaper or journal with seasoned journalists from that specific area. Also, the Internet can bring the world to your fingertips. A news story, coupled to your imagination (employing a bit of embellishment) when composing fiction, can offer a beginning, middle, and end. If the factual story falls short of your expectations, you simply say, "But what if . . . ? What if *this* occurred other than what actually happened?" No differently than I did by making Barry Shulman the monster and his brother, Robert, the fall guy. Don't sell yourself short. Forget TV. Referencing fiction, be your own programmer and write the words that you believe *your* audience wants to read.

The reinstatement of New York State's death penalty in 1995, followed by its repeal in 2004, figured significantly into two of my novels, *The Author* and *The Teacher*. The timing was perfect. As an underlying theme, that legislation helped pave the way for a series, with Justin Barnes at the top of his game. Seeing that the two novels became award winners, I'd say that I succeeded in building verisimilitude into those works, along with two more novels in the series to follow; namely, *Knots* and *The Good Samaritans*. Let's examine an example of Suffolk County Homicide sanctioning the elimination of Clarence Emery, a diabolical serial killer and protégé of Malcolm Columba, whom Justin Barnes had *dealt* with earlier in time. The following chapter is excerpted from *The Teacher*.

The Teacher
Chapter Seven [excerpt]

Detective Lieutenant Theodore Groche, Commanding Officer of the Suffolk County homicide squad in Yaphank, sat ill at ease behind his desk...thinking...its surface neatly organized into piles of paperwork. Several stacks stood to either side. File records, memorandums, and newspapers took up most of the remaining space.

Justin Barnes knocked, entered, then closed the door and crossed the room, planting a buttock upon the corner of the massive mahogany piece. He sat with his back to the floor-to-ceiling windowed wall that ran the length of the front office.

[**Note:** As covered in Lesson 4, **spatial description** is quite important in bringing believability to the scene. Accorded the honor and privilege of an interview with the commander of the Suffolk County Homicide Squad, I would make the most of it. On January 31st, 2001, I was escorted to the second floor area. Detectives were seated in a hallway behind their desks across from their commander's office. I was summarily summoned into Detective Lieutenant John Gierasch's sanctum. I took in my immediate surroundings—every square foot.]

"Take a chair," the lieutenant said absently, reaching for and opening a confidential file.

"Won't be staying long. Just wanted to report to you in person."

"She bite?"

"With her bare teeth. Snarled first with fair warning."

"Lay it out for her?"

"Never got the chance."

Theo yawned and stretched. "I was afraid of that. How far did you get?"

"Through the door of the restaurant and over to the bar area. Told her what we needed."

"And?"

"And she practically threw me out."

"Think she'll come around?"

Justin shrugged. "Maybe when she learns who the two women were and it has time to sink in."

"You didn't tell her?"

"Wouldn't 'ave mattered much at that point. She'll need time to sort things out. Digest some of the gruesome details. The fact that they were very good customers ain't gonna do it for her. Let her read it in the paper for herself rather than hear it from my mouth. I'll tell her later who was missing exactly what."

"Missing four quarts of blood wouldn't do it?"

Justin shook his head. "Trust me. I know how her mind works."

"Maybe *you* should get a job at Kirby. Then you could poison Emery yourself."

Justin smiled uneasily. "By the time I completed the application, he'd be gone."

"How?"

"He'll figure a way. Believe me."

Theo grinned and shook his head. "This is not the movies, J. Sure he could beat the death penalty if we don't stop him in his tracks, but he's not going anywhere."

"Really believe that?"

"I do."

"Then why are you sanctioning this business now?"

"Because of the nature of his violence. Because of the sheer number of young women whose lives he's taken. Main reason? Because he'd kill again *wherever* the state puts him."

"Not because he took the life of one of your own?" the maverick added to the mix.

Lieutenant Groche ignored the remark. "We got some time. But if you're right, and I'm not saying that you are, J—"

"You just wanna hedge your bet," Justin jabbed.

Theo looked up from the file and smiled. "Tell you what."

"What?"

"If he evaporates from Kirby, or points between there and prison before we pull the plug on this freak, I'll let you call the shots in hunting him down. How's that?"

"I want that in writing; in stone—or even parchment paper will do."

Theo put down the report and leaned forward, extending a bony hand. "This will have to do, J."

Justin stared at the lieutenant's spindly fingers. "I want you to take your finger and make a U in the center of my palm, boss."

"What for?"

"I told you. I want it in writing."

"Meaning?"

Justin just sat there grinning, exposing his pearly whites for all they were worth.

The commander laughed. "Meaning, 'U da man'?"

"You got it. This way you won't forget so easily." Justin held out a sizable mitt.

The lieutenant took it and drew an invisible U upon Justin's palm, then balled the black man's fingers into a fist. "There. Signed and sealed. How's that? Happy, now?"

"Either way, we're gonna deliver this fucker from evil. But if he boogies on outta there, can I wheel an' deal from behind that desk of yo's, bossman?" Justin questioned with a drawl, slipping into the role of his sassy, streetwise savvy self.

"Don't push it, cowboy."

"Oh, no sa. I's never ever do dat."

"Press is going to release the names and some new details concerning the Greenport victims tomorrow. Besides being a good customer at the Bella Sera, one of them went to grammar school with Jackie. Maybe you can try her again in the afternoon."

"Try her patience for sure."

"So, you never got to tell her how The Professor himself would call her in."

"Told her he'd invite her there for a visit if we gave him half a reason."

"Tell her again tomorrow. The newspapers will print what I give them and hold back what they may learn on their own...for now."

"Will do."

"Now get your black ass off my desk and go to work."

"Comments like dat be one o' da reasons why mos' my brothers choose unemployment, boss." Justin grinned broadly.

"You could be next in line yourself if you don't watch your step."

"And jus' what kind o' step dat be, bossman? Dat be a shuffle, o' a lazy-ass attitudinal sashay?"

"Don't matter much to me because we white guys just take you boys in stride."

"Say what?"

"Out. Got work to do." Theo set aside the file, then pulled a stack of papers in front of him.

"You know, Lieutenant? I got to thinking. I've got the best job in the world and get paid pretty well; eliminating white folk with a serious sort of social problem, like our professor there." He pointed down to the file. "Ever take notice that few black folk get caught up in this serial killer shit? Sure, we cause a lot of the crime. But we ain't fuckin' sick like that. Ever stop to think about that, boss?"

"I thought you weren't staying long. Your words."

"Yeah, and I got your word right here." Justin held up a palm like a catcher's mitt.

"You sure do. But first he's got to fly the coop like you believe he's going to do before 'U da man,' J," the man in charge reminded him with an impatient look.

Justin slid his backside off the lieutenant's desk and stood quietly.

Theo sighed. "What now?"

Justin tested. "Doesn't it bother you that she could possibly do some serious time?"

"Who?"

"Who. Jackie. That's who. Even if she pulled it off, she'd be suspected and maybe even indicted."

"Who's going to indict her?"

"Them." Justin gestured eastward toward the county seat. "D.A. and his entourage."

"*Them* is with us," the man put forth matter-of-factly.

"Maybe in another lifetime and some other jurisdiction."

"You're not around here long enough to know how things really work, J."

"Why don't you enlighten me so I can give her reassurance?"

"Maybe in time."

"Doesn't worry you, does it?"

"Worries you, I see. Otherwise, you would have pressed her a little harder. Hey, didn't we take care of everything last time out?"

"Right, boss." Justin nodded with a degree of satisfaction before taking his leave. "That you did."

****

Of course, it would take several such examples to convince readers that a commander of a homicide unit would actually authorize such a covert action. So, not only do I have to convince a reading audience that Justin Barnes has been brought into law enforcement's fold, but that a hierarchy, shrouded in secrecy, sanctions the serial killer's murder. Tall order, but I pull it off. How? Again, through several justifiable scenes and actions that paint a clear and plausible picture. That is the key. <u>Do not just tell</u> your readers that this is the way things are, <u>show them</u> by way of example, painting a series of clear pictures in their minds, continuously striving to build believability into your scenes.

In the next lesson, we'll explore a scene to bolster those themes, which might not have proved plausible had I not *illuminated* the actions of Justin Barnes and Suffolk County Homicide.

LESSON 6

COMPLEXITIES CONCERNING CHARACTERIZATION AND PLOT

Human beings are oftentimes complicated. Accordingly, your fictional characters *may* be more or less intricate. However, a writer new to the novel should craft his or her plot (storyline) in a straightforward fashion that is relatively free from complexities. But to create both complex characterization and an entangled plot is to flirt with disaster because you run the risk of losing your reader. That should be a newcomer's biggest concern. Therefore, do not tax your readers; do not put them or yourself on overload.

In my novel titled *Knots* (third in a four-book series), I present a singular theme tied to underlying motifs found in *The Author* and *The Teacher*: Justin Barnes' indoctrination into Suffolk County's Homicide Unit; the reinstatement of New York State's death penalty in 1995; its repeal in 2004; and Homicide's sanctioning the murder of certain serial killers. The subject matter in *Knots* addresses the cloning of human beings. The novel is not to be considered science fiction, for the story is based on facts—as you will see in a moment. Being that the storyline is somewhat elaborate, I kept my characters (with one exception) on an even keel so as not to detract from the main focus: cloning. Certainly, the mind of a serial killer is complex as is the applied science of DNA and technology referencing cloning; therefore, I work within those parameters by taking great pains in presenting ostensibly heady material and putting it on a level that a layperson can comprehend. Tall order? Perhaps for a first novel, but keep in mind that I am building a series. My readers know Justin Barnes intimately and most of the major characters. I can now have readers concentrate on the matter at hand—cloning.

Of course, I have to sell this book idea to a literary agent or publisher; hence, my query letter offering the agent or publisher a brief synopsis. Note that I presented the letter of introduction in the form of a bio, keeping it to one page; the synopsis to three pages.

Robert Banfelder

Knots (manuscript form) Robert Banfelder
141 Riverside Drive
Riverhead, NY 11901-2451
(631) 369-3192

KNOTS
Word Count: 73,400
Bio

E-mail: robertbanfelder@gmail.com
Website: www.robertbanfelder.com

Date ——

Dear ——,

Bio

My first novel titled *No Stranger Than I* (later published as *Dicky, Richard, and I*) was published in 1991. It is a story of madness in the making and was reviewed as a "brilliant" psychological thriller. I followed that up with two award-winning novels: *The Author* and *The Teacher*. Both works are serial killer thrillers and part of a four-book series. *Knots*, which is the third book in the series, is outlined in the attached synopsis.

Early in my career, I was a crime reporter for a small Queens, New York newspaper, having written extensive editorials that resulted in the release of an innocent young man from prison. Conversely, I helped put a guilty lad away for murder. Also, I taught college English and Creative Writing classes for thirteen years as an adjunct lecturer. Presently, I freelance outdoors articles as well as pursuing my fiction writing full time.

Additionally, I give talks/lectures on topics such as the phenomenon of the serial killer, exploring the criminal mind, FBI profiling, and the writing process. After having attended the fifteen-month long Robert Shulman serial killer trial in Riverhead, New York, I was asked to lecture before students and faculty at Kirby Forensic Psychiatric Center (for the criminally insane) on Ward's Island in Manhattan. In 2001, I interviewed Suffolk County's Homicide Commander, Detective Lieutenant John Gierasch. The Shulman serial killer trial, coupled to several interviews, led to my novel titled *Trace Evidence*. Also, I have appeared on Cablevision's *Literally Speaking* and *Off the Cuff*, speaking on related topics. Rather than go on incessantly, please visit my expansive website at www.robertbanfelder.com.

My manuscript, *Knots*, is ready to be sent to you, pending your request. Thank you in advance for your time, and I look forward to hearing from you.

Sincerely,
Robert Banfelder
Enclosure: SASE

[**Note:** If you are sending off a synopsis separately, you still need a cover letter to introduce yourself. I chose to combine a letter of introduction with a bio as covered above. If you have credentials, flaunt them. It's a poor dog that can't wag its own tail. If you have simply queried a literary agent or publisher to see if they might be interested in your work, and they ask for a synopsis, keep it to two or three pages unless you are instructed otherwise. Here is an example of a synopsis for *Knots*. Due to the nature of the novel, its theme being cloning, I felt it was imperative to immediately point out that although it is a work of fiction the story is tightly based on facts. Too, I want the agent/publisher to note that this is a third novel in a four-book series.]

Robert Banfelder

Knots (manuscript form) Robert Banfelder
141 Riverside Drive
Riverhead, NY 11901-2451
(631) 369-3192
E-mail: robertbanfelder@gmail.com
Website: www.robertbanfelder.com

KNOTS
Word Count: 73,400
Synopsis

Date ——

Dear —— ,

    First an important note: *Knots* is my third novel in an award-winning series. The story takes place in 2003, and in real time parallels the existent company, Clonaid Inc.—a self-described human cloning company associated with the Raelian Movement—a current religious sect that sees cloning as the pathway to immortality. Therefore, my novel is not loosely based on Clonaid and the Raelian Movement, but rather solidly built on facts and firmly implanted in the fictional account. I renamed Clonaid Inc., Clonite, Inc. and the Raelian Movement, Reality, Ltd. *Knots* follows my two earlier award-winning works: *The Author* and its sequel *The Teacher*, published in 2006 and 2007. My antagonist in *Knots*, Kalvin Matheson, is enamored by the deadly acts of serial killers Malcolm Columba and Clarence Emery. Columba and Emery were portrayed in *The Author* and *The Teacher*, respectively. The two serial killers, working in concert, were terminated by my protagonist, Justin Barnes, an African-American maverick operating covertly for Suffolk County Homicide in Yaphank, New York.

Synopsis

Saddened by the recent murders of Kalvin Matheson's (antagonist) two dearly departed serial killer "pals" (Malcolm Columba and Clarence Emery), the madman embarks on a single-minded mission to follow in his heroes' footsteps. Kalvin Matheson's ultimate goal is to have his identical twin brother, Alvin, and himself cloned. Coupled to the advancements in groundbreaking technology are promises made to Kalvin by both Reality, Ltd. and its parent company, Clonite, Inc.—promises of everlasting life!

Whereas Reality borders on the lunatic fringe, Clonite is well-respected and immersed in mainstream science. Clonite is on the brink of success, having supposedly cloned the first human being. Consequently, Reality is taking on a new dimension—one of unparalleled proportion. A one-time, up-front, ground-floor fee of one million dollars guarantees a person the promise of everlasting life, though one must patiently wait for the technology to be further developed and the procedure perfected. The proverbial pot is sweetened by Bishop John, of the Reality Church, who offers Kalvin a two-for-one deal for everlasting life: Kalvin and Alvin. Consequently, bodies suddenly expire—involving insurance schemes perpetrated by the out-of-work insurance salesman in an attempt to raise one million dollars. Meanwhile, Kalvin Matheson has both his and Alvin's healthy, living cells stored safely in one of Clonite's laboratories.

Clonite has been supporting Reality with dollars and a propaganda machine for almost forty years. The enormous success behind the company's as well as the church's operation is founded on *faith*. No longer is the possibility of cloning a human being steeped in some sort of mystic belief or myth. "A human clone has been created," or so Clonite is telling the world. But a faction within the scientific community believes that the company cannot—at this point in time—deliver. Skeptics feel that Clonite will be unable to furnish DNA proof of such a claim, believing that in the penultimate hour the alleged parents of the clone will not submit to tests for fear the courts would take the child away, or excuses along those lines.

As time goes by and more bodies turn up, there are tenuous similarities between old homicides and the current crime scenes. Police authorities have good reason to believe that both Malcolm Columba and Clarence Emery were deeply involved with both Clonite and the Reality Church. Authorities must acquire the church's member list as well as Clonite's confidential and well-guarded client list, hoping that the information will lead them to their serial killer's identity. However, Reality's member list is kept as secret as Clonite's laboratories and client list. Therefore, Suffolk County Homicide detectives figure a way to infiltrate both organizations.

Eventually, a suspect is ultimately brought in for questioning, and Kalvin Matheson reveals a truth that reflects his sickness of mind. However, at that juncture, authorities cannot prove Matheson's guilt. When guilt is finally established, Justin Barnes (protagonist), a covert operative for Suffolk County Homicide, shares a concern with a faction of Suffolk County Homicide's Team Three unit. The deranged yet extremely clever killer will undoubtedly be declared insane and one day set free to kill again and again. The Team deems extreme action necessary and justified. While the serial killer is in custody, Justin and select members of Team Three scheme to affect Matheson's demise.

What is ultimately important to Kalvin Matheson is that Clonite, Inc. packages and provides *immortality* for both him and his brother as promised by the bishop. Hope springs eternal in the madman's mind as Kalvin is the last of his ancestral line.

Kalvin has committed murders not only for money but for the *thrill* of it (as do *all* serial killers). Homicide detectives had followed clues that lead them down a primrose path to the hour in which they arrest their prime suspect, only to learn that the madman is actually his twin brother, Alvin—not Kalvin. Justin learns that Alvin Matheson had his own brother, Kalvin, killed.

In the final hour, members of Team Three and Justin win out over a hierarchy that has sanctioned such covert operations in the past but is now adamant to authorize similar action anew. Justin cleverly devises a way in which Alvin Matheson will take his own life while in police custody, ironically hanging himself in a fashion befitting a consummate executor of *Knots*.

****

[**Note:** In a synopsis, you have to spell out virtually everything to the agent or publisher, including a surprise ending as evidenced the synopsis. Yes, you have to give it away. Think back to the lesson referencing Shirley Jackson's *The Lottery*. I had revealed the shocking conclusion before we read that short story. The agent or publisher has to know the whole deal. Be reminded to keep the synopsis to two or three pages. Of course, you will follow the agent's or publisher's guidelines to a T.]

Detective Lieutenant John Gierasch, commander of the Suffolk County Homicide Squad, now retired, became the template for Detective Lieutenant Theodore Groche, featured through a four-book fictionalized series. When Theo retires and a new commander is appointed to the homicide unit, politics rears its ugly head and becomes a major issue. You can have a field day by *showing*, those interpersonal and often explosive relationships. The following is excerpted from *Knots*. The **dènouement**, the unraveling of plot, is at the threshold of the new commander's office. Enjoy the uninterrupted read:

Knots
Chapter Fifty-Six [excerpt]

Within minutes, Yaphank's infamous prisoner was taken from the interrogation room and booked. The serial killer's prints were processed and immediately sent through AFIS: Automated Fingerprint Identification Systems.

Deputy Inspector Sean O'Leary, along with Detectives Brian and Kim Archer, Gary York, Yolanda Ivers, and Xavier Valez, had listened in astonishment to Matheson's taped confession. As to which Matheson, Kalvin or Alvin, the police retained, remained a mystery for the moment. It was evident that the six individuals had been arguing. Heatedly.

Justin knocked upon and immediately opened the door to Detective Lieutenant Powell's office. He stood in the doorway, taking in the brood of sullen faces. "I just faxed a report along with a copy of the drawing off to Lancaster P.D. They're on it," he announced, stepping inside and off to a corner.

"You live in a barn, Barnes?" the deputy inspector snapped.

"Used to. A few of them, in fact." Justin reached over and closed the door. "But now that I'm so high and mighty—zoom!—*el·e·va·tor* right to my new penthouse apartment in a mostly integrated neighborhood. Mastic/Shirley." The maverick grinned. "Doors open and close *au·to·mat·i·cal·ly* for *moi*, via an electric eye—*pho·to·cell*—so I have this tendency to forget."

"How you spend your money is your business, Barnes."

"Down in the lobby, we got us a white knight," Justin jawed away. "Doorman sportin' a blue cap and matching coat with brass buttons. I couldn't help but notice that you got yourself one o' them ceramic ceremonial sambos standin' 'longside your driveway—holdin' up one of those 'lectric lanterns, Inspector. But I never, ever see it lit on those evenings when you come home late. You should, though. Just can't be too careful nowadays, you know. Cop or no cop."

O'Leary stood up from behind Powell's desk and walked brashly up to Justin. "Are you threatening me?"

"A Suffolk County deputy inspector? You think I'm crazy?"

"I catch you *anywhere* near my house, day or night, I'll thrash you. Got that?"

"Catch me doin' what?"

"You stay out of my neighborhood. Hear?"

"Well, you're welcome in mine any ol' time, Inspector. Course you might not make it out in one pi—"

Kim placed a hand over Justin's mouth. "Save it, J."

"No, let him say what he has to say," O'Leary challenged. "Hey! Tough guy. Just remember. I know firsthand how you made your money before you ever came aboard here."

"Really? I never figured you for a crackhead. Or was it one of my *fine* lady friends who entertained you for an evening every now and then—huh? And I thought I knew *all* their johns. Ah, I'll bet *you're* the guy they talk about who sticks that rug you wear between your legs for laughs. Yeah. The one the Asian girls call F*ruzzy*?"

O'Leary's face was beet red. "You're only here because of Theo Groche, Barnes," the inspector blew, pointing to a picture on the wall of homicide's recently retired commanding officer. "But that's drawing to a close—and soon. Powell's got his eye on you, I want you to know."

"And my baby browns on him as well," Justin mocked in an affected, effeminate manner and tone, standing toe-to-toe before the man. "Nice cheeks on that boy, too. Rather big, but *ni·ice*, nevertheless," he babbled away gaily as Brian moved him back a step.

"You're fuckin' sick, Barnes. Know that?"

"Or maybe you'd like to inspect this, Inspector," Justin jawed, grabbing his crotch and blowing the man a kiss. "I think that's your *pre·di·lec·tion* and desired *po·si·tion*. I say that because F*ruzzy* never really got it on with the ladies. He'd just like to drink warm sake while jerking off into his hairpiece in a dark closet. Know where the term wigger really comes from, Sean?"

"You're on report!" the inspector flared.

"Sorry, deputy, but I don't exist. So take your tin and shove it where the sun don't shine." Justin turned to Gary. "Line from some western long forgotten," he whispered, bringing a limp wrist to his brow in contemplation. "I'm trying to think who was in it, but I can't because they were all white."

Brian had had it and interceded. "Enough clowning around, J! We've all got work to do."

"And I said we're not moving on this till we match his prints," the inspector affirmed.

"I thought they can determine I.D. in a matter of minutes," Yolanda said in exasperation.

"Normally, they can," Kim explained. "But someone please tell me what's normal about this case? Even AFIS has its limitations. We're dealing with identical twins that have similar arch patterns, loops, and whorls. A trained examiner, not a computer, will have the last word, Yolanda. Hence, the delay."

"Well, I don't think it makes a goddamn bit of difference if that's Kalvin, Alvin, or Attila the Hun in there," Yolanda's partner, Xavier, fumed. "We got the guy who did the deed; and in this case, at least seven victims that we now know about. We got his confession on tape, thanks to J. We got a detailed drawing, in Matheson's own hand, of where he put Passaro's body. What happened to our agreement? Huh, Inspector?"

O'Leary ran his eyes over everyone. "The problem, my insubordinate renegades, is a tricky legal one that's plagued our judicial system since the dawn of modern madness. Insanity versus sanity. To which warehouse do the courts send these people? The nuthouse or the jailhouse? And now with the death penalty back on the books, we further complicate and compound matters. If that's truly Alvin and not Kalvin in there, do we execute a deranged man who the doctors as well as the courts deemed certifiable more than a decade ago? A lunatic who spent a good part of his life in mental hospitals."

"We're not executing anyone. We're just giving him the means to expedite matters for himself."

"Do you hear yourself, Kim Archer?" O'Leary snapped. "That's not an unbiased professional talking. You're taking this very personally because one of the victims happened to be your goddaughter."

"For openers, if that's Alvin we have back there, which I believe it is, he spent a good part of his life as a free animal. Free to torture, torment, and murder men, women and children. We don't know *how* many people he's actually killed, while his innocent brother rotted away inside a mental hospital."

"Tell the inspector why you think that it's Alvin we're holding back there, Kim," Yolanda proposed.

"Because Alvin Matheson was an electrician's helper whenever he did work, which accounts for how he knew to rig the golf cart with an electric heat gun applicator to finish off Vivian. Also, the way he strung Emily Schroeder's body from the ceiling fixture with electrical cord. Remember how neatly the connections were spliced? Not to mention the fact that he ran the electric that lights the steps leading up and down Chris and Harriet's spiral staircase."

"And what if it is Alvin Matheson? Why can't we move this ahead as planned?" Gary pressed. "Is it really any different? So what if we're dealing with a split personality or a multiple personality or whatever. What's the goddamn point? Maybe Alvin's a very good actor. Or maybe Kalvin's really the actor. Who cares? I say we move this along now. Let him end it himself. Whoever it is in there, Alvin or Kalvin, he's not going to wait around for the rest of his natural life, or sit on death row for a decade, or hang his hat on the hook of hope for years awaiting the outcome, expecting to land on his feet in some loony bin in lieu of receiving a lethal injection. This guy sees the proverbial bright light at the end of a very short tunnel. But more importantly, we'd be giving Chris and Harriet closure today rather than some future tomorrow. We owe them that much. We'd be doing them, ourselves, and the public a favor now rather than enduring hearing after hearing followed by a lengthy and expensive trial. We're simply the ways and means committee, Inspector."

"Oh, you're good, Gary. I give you that. I see why they call you the closer. But I want all of you to think about this. If we allow ourselves to let him commit suicide—this sick-minded man—we have to live with our conscience till the end of our own days."

"Our conscience?" Brian laughed.

"Yes, our conscience, damn it."

"Define that."

"Define what?"

"Conscience, Inspector. If I'm going to live with something for the rest of my days, I want to know exactly what it is I'm dealing with."

"Come on, Brian. The awareness of what is simply *right* and *wrong*. The *awareness*," he repeated. "Otherwise, we're no better than any of them that pass through our doors."

"Why don't we take a vote and see exactly where we all stand on this matter?" Xavier suggested.

"You see, Detective," the inspector said while exhibiting a good degree of condescension and body language, "you're still young yet. You just can't view this whole business as a single picture. You have to examine each piece of the mosaic. Alvin as an escapee from a mental hospital, if that be the case. Kalvin as a split personality. Actor, or genuinely disturbed. Slick or sick. You simply do not harm, or cause to bring about harm to a sick-minded individual, Detective Xavier Valez. Period."

Justin had to laugh. "Just a moment ago you said that *I* was sick. And what did you want to do to me? Thrash me, or worse. So, with all *un*due respect, I got you figured like this, Inspector. You're prejudiced, you're jealous, and you're afraid of the fallout from a full-blown investigation if either Alvin or Kalvin takes his life on your watch because no one will be watching the prisoner as he takes the *E-ZPass*. Well, I'm not going to stand around here and placate anyone by picking apart this and that. I refuse to suffer the paralysis of analysis. No, sir. Not me. I choose to lump all this shit together because it all *belongs* on a single plate. It doesn't really matter to me at all whether it's Kalvin or Alvin in there, whether he's sick or slick or deserves an Academy Award. That man in there, whoever the fuck he is, admitted to killing seven human beings with malice aforethought. He's not some babbling idiot who picked up a hatchet thinking it was a compress to help relieve his mother's migraine. He calculated and planned those murders to a T. Mr. Matheson. That's *my* mosaic. I choose to see the big and complete picture, Inspector. Not all the little squares."

Kim, Brian, Yolanda, Xavier, and Gary gave Justin a standing round of applause.

"You're a fine one to talk, Barnes," O'Leary snapped. "A stone-cold killer in your own right. I've read your record. The one that doesn't exist. Every paragraph and page. You're actually a disgrace to this department and its teams of fine detectives, this county, this state—the entire country, in fact."

"Ah, but you do haveta admit I cover a lot of ground."

"Great men like Theodore Groche and Ethan Powell have been blindsided by your results, Barnes. But results without conscience makes for a shallow, hollow shell of a man. And like a cancer, you've corrupted several good men and women like Brian and Kim, Gary, Xavier, and Yolanda. Corrupted them with your evil ways."

"My God, man! And where do you fit in along the line, Inspector?" Kim asked in amazement. "Part of your problem is that you sit behind that desk of yours and wield power from another world while we're down here in the trenches. You've earned that right, God knows. See, I've read *your* record. But to come down here with your platitudes and attitudes and pass judgment, when you don't even know this man, is unfair."

"Unfair? I know all I need to know. I've dealt with a thousand smart ass punks like Barnes, up through the ranks and down through the years. He's no different than any of them. The only reason I went along with this business, up to a point, is because of circumstances. But the circumstances have changed. Haven't they, Kim? You don't take the law into your own hands."

"Oh, but *you* and the higher-ups can and do exactly that. You play God when it's convenient. That's why Justin was brought on board in the first place."

"There are certain circumstances. Yes."

"And this is one of them."

"It is, if and when I say it is. And I say we wait and see exactly what we're dealing with."

"By then it may be too late."

"Dem's the breaks, kid." The inspector smirked.

"Once the county jail gets a hold of him, we're dead in the water. I want this fucker stopped. Now!"

"Now, you just stop it, Kim. All of you! I didn't want to get into a rather sensitive area, but I see I have no choice. It starts with you and Brian. It ends with Barnes, as it always does. Gary, Yolanda, and Xavier are stuck in the middle of this mess. I'm trying to stop all of you from making a terrible mistake, here. I'm trying to save your careers. Take your fucking blinders off, folks. Take the wax out of your ears. Look, listen, and learn. Osip fucked up. All right? He fucked up with those pics and reports, and he fucked up with his daughter. You were godmother to Vivian, Kim. Vivian's dead. Brian. You are Chris' friend. Right away we got a bad batch brewing. Friends of the family, and conflicts of interest." Sean O'Leary shook his head sadly. "Gary. You're Brian's partner. Yolanda and Xavier. You two worked this case closely with those in this room. You're *all* too personally involved. See the big picture as Barnes puts it? And because I sit behind a desk at a distance from all of you, I have a much clearer perspective. If you take away these elements, this intimacy if you will, this Alvin/Kalvin killer is a boy scout compared to Malcolm Columba and Clarence Emery. Matheson is just your garden variety serial killer. Like it or not."

"This garden variety psychopath is a Columba/Emery emulator whose collecting all their merit badges in case you haven't noticed," Kim hammered away.

"From where you're sitting, I suppose so, Kim."

"So, we're supposed to sit on our hands and wait? I know what's going to happen. We all know what's going to happen. We'll wait for the print match. Then we'll wait for a psychiatric evaluation. And then we'll wait to see if this goes to trial or if he's shipped off to a hospital."

"She's right," Gary said. "Three death penalty cases in this county in the past several years. Can Suffolk even afford another? It would be cheaper in the long run if we recruited more covert operatives like Justin. Believe-you-me."

"Consultant, if you please," Justin underscored.

"Consultant. Covert operative, my ass," O'Leary rejoined. "Suffolk County's stone-cold killing machine would be calling a spade a spade. One of you, Barnes, is too many if you ask me. If I had my say, you'd be long gone."

"You know, it's not like J's going in and blowing the guy's head off," Yolanda contended. "He's simply handing the man his coat and saying *adiós*."

"*Hasta la vista*," Xavier added

"*Hasta luego*," Yolanda concluded, waving her fingers in a final farewell.

"It's like I started telling the inspector a moment ago," Justin interjected. "In my new upscale neighborhood and lingo it's sayonara, muthafucker. Don't really matter what your creed or code. You know, I even got me a samurai sword hanging over the couch. I'm telling you, culture-wise, I'm really getting into the swing of things. Not the Mau Mau I use to be, brothers and sisters. No siree."

The inspector stared at Justin for what seemed like an eternity. Finally, he spoke. "You've heard nothing of what I've said here, Barnes. But I want you to hear what I'm saying now. And that is, I don't like you at all."

"Oh, now *that's* a fucking surprise!" Justin turned to Brian and whispered. "That's a line from *My Cousin Vinny*, you know. After Fred Gwynne as the judge turns to Joe Pesci playing Vinny, and tells him he's going to find him in contempt and that—"

The phone rang. O'Leary snapped it up. "Yeah . . . Uh-huh . . . Right . . . No, I understand perfectly . . . All right . . . Thank you." He set the receiver down upon its cradle as if he were putting a wee infant to bed.

The five detectives were at a loss to read the deputy inspector's poker face.

Justin just scratched his nose. "Well, was I right as usual?"

"It's Alvin Matheson," O'Leary finally said. "Kalvin's sign-in signature of his last visit to his brother at Pilgrim State was forged and matches Alvin's handwriting. Kalvin Matheson died in his sleep in that institution five years later—buried as Alvin Matheson. Fingerprints, too, confirm we're holding Alvin Frederick Matheson."

"They even shared the same middle name," Yolanda said.

"And all Alvin had to do was add a K to his given name and assume his brother's identity," Kim added, shaking her head in wonder. "A role which he played brilliantly."

"K for killer," Gary affirmed.

"So, how do we stand, Inspector?" Xavier asked. "Or you just wanna stand around here and beat up on us some more?"

O'Leary turned about like a turret and took aim at the detective's questions. "You're right, Xavier. The moment of truth is at hand. The time has come for me to make a final decision. The truth of the matter is . . . I can't. Not without losing my soul versus losing five good detectives who threaten to mutiny or walk or whatever." He paused and sighed sorrowfully. "So, here's what I propose," he continued, dipping a hand deep into a pant pocket. "No matter how silly it may sound." O'Leary produced a silver coin. A quarter. "If I'm forced to make a definitive and final decision, it's going to be that we hand Alvin Matheson over to the courts. You can count on it. But first, I'd order you to remove the item from the lining of his coat, Barnes. If, however, I flip this coin and lose the toss, you may proceed, realizing, of course, that Alvin Matheson may not comply with your wishes anyway. In which case, it'll be the same as my having won the toss. Then, if he takes his life at some later point in time, without anyone here helping him along the way, you'll all have a clear conscience. The flip of this coin decides his fate. Not us, exactly. What do you say?"

The six knew they had but little choice. Left to the discretion of O'Leary, the matter would be completely out of their control. On the other hand, there was a fifty-fifty chance they might have their way.

The five detectives formed a huddle.

Justin Barnes and Inspector O'Leary exchanged formidable stares.

Seconds later, the team's quarterback spoke up. "I want to see that coin; and *I* make the toss," Brian said.

But the inspector smiled and shook his head. "Barnes has the honors." He handed over the coin for examination. "High in the air and you let it fall to the carpet. Heads, Alvin Matheson heads for arraignment. Tails, it's a question of destiny. Fair?"

Justin took and examined both sides of the coin then nodded. "Funny. We be *The Magnificent Seven*. You, Sean, be da man. But good ol' G. W., here, could beat us to the punch. If that don't beat all." Suddenly, a thumbnail shot the quarter upward from beneath a cocked forefinger, sending the silvery item end over end, missing the ceiling by a fraction before falling to the blue-green carpeting.

****

[**Note:** You know from the synopsis that the police eventually sanction the serial killer's suicide and that Justin and Team Three are instrumental, assisting in Alvin Matheson's demise. However, you do not know exactly *how* this was brought about, except that the end result was that the killer hanged himself. That is what I mean by revealing virtually everything to the agent/publisher. You must explain the storyline and its outcome, not necessarily how you arrived at that juncture. You have to pique the in-house reader's curiosity; he or she may be some summer student intern or the actual head of the agency. You just never know. Therefore, make your cover letter salient but not complex. Your synopsis must be powerfully packaged. Having sparked curiosity, hopefully, you will be asked to send several chapters or the entire manuscript.]

In tying up loose ends concerning the complexities involving characterization and plot, let's turn to the foundation of those elements: the single sentence. Two common faults to avoid in constructing your prose are redundancy and repetitiveness, defined here in the following sense. Redundancy: Excessive wordiness in a single sentence tends to cloud expression. Repetitiveness: The repetition of the same word in a single sentence or even a paragraph can become tedious. Take the time to find a synonym rather than repeat the same word. A thesaurus should be close at hand, preferably next to your unabridged dictionary. These are two tools of paramount importance.

Review your prose to see if you have committed these serious missteps. While you are there, read your work aloud. Your ears will catch most of what your eyes miss. Trust me on these important points.

LESSON 7

Contextual, Grammatical, and Syntactical Problems That Plague Writers ~ Part I
AKA "Got any Gum?"

I remember, vividly, sitting and shuddering in *grammar* school, fearful that the teacher would call on me to point out or define such elements as nouns, verbs, subjects, adverbs, adjectives, et cetera. No sooner than I finally had part of the puzzle figured out, I was suddenly transferred to another school where the teacher used a different format to teach those parts of speech. The method she used is commonly referred to as diagramming sentences. To me, at that tender age, it might just as well have been a crash course in deciphering hieroglyphics or Chinese. It took me awhile (not a while) to learn that an adverb had something to do with a verb because this new teacher called them predicates. I disliked grammar, *grammar* school, and English as a subject (seemingly a second language), for whoever heard of direct or indirect objects? Additionally, I disliked several of my English teachers—two of whom spoke with an accent and scrawled on the blackboard like a chicken scratching in the dirt. This certainly complicated matters . . . significantly, for me. If anyone had told me during my formative years that I would one day become an English teacher, instructing college English, no less, I'd have laughed in his or her face. I became a college English instructor by way of my desire to pursue creative writing. I soon realized that I had to know a bit more than basic grammar before I would, if ever, become a successful writer, let alone a college professor.

What to do?

I did something that changed my life. I taught *myself* the fundamentals of grammar. Along the way, however, I had one exceptional English teacher. That remarkable instructor, ironically, was a retired professional basketball player. Go figure.

Years later, right before I found myself attending college English composition courses, I hit the books—hard. In sheer frustration, I even threw one grammar book against a wall. Convoluted, confusing, contradictory and, therefore, unclear were the adjectives I would use to describe some of these poorly worded texts. Yet, in each textbook, I was able to at least get the gist of the conundrum. By going through a number of grammar texts, covering and comparing one particular element at a time, I was finally able to obtain a very clear picture of what otherwise proved to be rather narrow or obtuse instruction as was presented in a single grammar guide. Still, problems persisted when one exercise in a particular text contradicted a lesson presented in another. I soon learned that there are so-called 'rules' that are *not* written in stone. I discovered, too, that there are esoteric arguments concerning grammar that are of little, if any, cognitive value, either presented upon the page or discussed in the classroom, other than to note that differences of opinion among professionals in that field of study do, indeed, exist. The English language is continuously evolving, yet there are hard-and-fast rules that do apply to grammar and *are* set in stone. To violate these elements is an unforgivable offense, and you will not be taken seriously by professionals.

What you will be presented with shortly are cogent rules to be followed that will lead to clear and concise writing, unquestionably recognized by professional educators and editors of the discipline. It is not my intent to turn you into a grammarian. My purpose is to turn you into a fine writer of prose, a person who has absolute confidence and a capital (not capitol) command of the English language. Everything is easy once you know how. Over the course of decades, I have consolidated the very best of *my* lessons and incorporated them into a comprehensible format. Said another way, this will be a cakewalk (in the informal sense) if you take this one step at a time, working at your own pace.

Let's take a good look at a multitude of mistakes that afflict many writers—mistakes that make you look bad. Mistakes and carelessness can, of course, be corrected. Ignorance (lacking knowledge) is a disease that if not treated through awareness and training will prove epidemic—an incurable pestilence spreading through page after page. At this juncture, we will review a few exercises in order to reinforce some of the important lessons that have been covered thus far. Also, we will build upon this sound foundation so as to thwart the spread of other infectious maladies that impair well-written prose.

Ready? Let's begin.

Dialogue tags: Once again, if a dialogue tag is not a <u>verb of speech</u>, as in the following example, one approach would be to divide the sentence in two.

Incorrect: "It's good of you to see me, Jimmy," Professor Emery grinned maniacally.

grinned is not a verb of speech

Correct: "It's good of you to see me, Jimmy." Professor Emery grinned maniacally.

The above has been divided into two sentences.

In order to correctly connect (tag) the above into a single sentence, the writer must employ a verb of speech such as said, asked, stated, confirmed, et cetera.

Correct: "It's good of you to see me, Jimmy," Professor Emery said.

or

The writer may add grinning maniacally because grinning maniacally is preceded by the verb of speech said.

Correct: "It's good of you to see me, Jimmy," Professor Emery said, grinning maniacally.

Just be sure to use the gerund (-ing form of the verb grin) grinning manically, preceded by a comma; otherwise, the professor is actually *saying* the words grinning maniacally instead of indicating the action of grinning maniacally.

This is a good place to introduce proper punctuation so that you will have, once and for all, complete confidence in writing a variety of sentences. Beginning with a simple grammatical unit, we will steadily build upon that foundation until you can handle even the most sophisticated of sentences. This is a most invaluable lesson in which you will learn how to avoid run-on sentences, comma splices, and fragments. These three fiends, without a doubt, haunt many, many writers. Those indefensible mistakes are the hallmark of amateurishness and will prevent you from being taken seriously by many professionals in the field of writing. You owe it to yourself to clean up these bedeviling demons immediately.

Forming a simple sentence:

Simple Sentence = 1 main clause
Theo hit a home run.

A simple sentence is a sentence having a single main clause. A main clause is a group of related words that contains at least one subject-verb unit. Let's examine this simple sentence. Theo hit a home run. What is the subject of this sentence? What is the verb of this sentence? We'll get there in just a moment, but first we are going to learn to boil water before we learn how to cook.

Understanding basic sentence structure:

In order to simplify identifying parts of a sentence, it is best to first find the heart of a sentence. The heart will lead you to the rest of the body. We'll begin by going hunting, figuratively speaking. We're on safari, a hunting expedition into Africa. We are deep in the jungle when suddenly the king of its domain comes into view. The 550-pound male cat appears out of a thicket, making its way downwind, along the edge of a grassy plain, stalking a band of bush beaters busy pursuing a wounded lioness through thick cover. The group of natives is unaware of the imminent danger lying just behind them.

The animal has paused momentarily. *You* have a clear broadside target. Where do you align the crosshairs of your telescopic sight—upon the beast's head? Do you take aim along its neck beneath its tawny mane? Or are you trained in drawing a vertical line up the big cat's foreleg and *slightly* rearward, holding along a horizontal plane perceived halfway between its spine and brisket (lower chest) for a heart shot? As the latter choice presents a larger target, leaving more of a forgiving margin of error, you would aim for the vitals—a deadly heart/lung shot.

Now, let's deal with the first clause in this two clause sentence [Theo hit a home run,] and the spectators cheered wildly. In hunting for and identifying parts of a sentence, the clear choice is to hunt for the heart. The heart of a sentence is the verb.

First clause: Theo hit a home run.

The above is a simple sentence because it is a main clause that contains a subject and verb. What is the subject of this sentence? Is it Theo? Is it hit? Or is it a home run? Remember, in order to identify the subject of a sentence, it is best to aim for the heart of the sentence; in other words, the verb. Most of us are familiar with verbs that express action. The action verb in this simple sentence is, obviously, hit. The word hit shows the action executed in this simple sentence.

Next, ask yourself who or what did the hitting? Did Theo do the hitting, or did a home run do the hitting? Clearly, Theo did the hitting. Therefore, the subject in this simple sentence is Theo.

Compound Sentence = 1 main clause + 1 main clause (that is, 2 main clauses)

Correct: Theo hit a home run, and the spectators cheered wildly.

A compound sentence is a sentence having two main clauses. A main clause is a group of related words that contains at least one subject-verb unit. Let's examine this compound sentence. [Theo hit a home run,] and [the spectators cheered wildly.] What is the subject and verb found in each clause?

We have already established that hit is the verb and that the subject is Theo in the first clause.

In the second clause [the spectators cheered wildly], we first hunt for the verb. The action verb in this compound sentence is cheered. Next, we ask ourselves who or what did the cheering in order to find the subject. Obviously, the spectators did the cheering. Hence, spectators is the subject in our second clause.

Now, here comes the magic. In combining the first and second clause, which forms our compound sentence, it is the comma [,] immediately preceding the word and that correctly *cements* the two clauses.

Correct: Theo hit a home run, and the spectators cheered wildly.

If you leave the comma out, you have committed a run-on sentence. Note that a run-on sentence is a misnomer because it is *not* a sentence that goes on forever as the name may imply. A run-on sentence is a sentence that is not punctuated correctly. James Joyce wrote a sentence that went on for almost thirty pages; it was not a run-on because it was punctuated correctly.

The following are seven pieces of cement that combine compound sentences. You need to know them like you know your ABCs. You do not need to remember that they are called coordinating conjunctions. You do need to know that they combine sentences that would otherwise cause choppy and, consequently, boring writing.

> and
> or
> but
> nor
> for
> so
> yet

Need an acronym to help you remember? Try **f a n b o y s**:

> **f**or
> **a**nd
> **n**or
> **b**ut
> **o**r
> **y**et
> **s**o

Whether you learn these connectors by rote or remember them via a set phrase, it behooves you to know them well.

Let's see what the writing would look and/or sound like if it were read aloud in this staccato-like fashion.

Avoid choppy writing:

Awkward, choppy writing: Theo hit a home run. The spectators cheered wildly. One person in the stands stood. He reached high. He caught the ball in his fielder's mitt. The sound echoed throughout the stadium.

As each piece of cement is employed differently, let's see how all seven coordinators [and, or, but, nor, for, so, yet] function in the following sentences.

Theo hit the ball, <u>and</u> he ran to first base.
Theo could smack the ball, <u>or</u> he could bunt.
Theo enjoys baseball, <u>but</u> he loves golf.
Theo does not watch basketball, <u>nor</u> does he view football.

Theo was sad, <u>for</u> the ballgame was cancelled.
Theo relaxes when fly-fishing, <u>so</u> he goes as often as he can.
Theo works a long day, <u>yet</u> he finds time to play.

You will note that the two clauses in each of the previous sentences show a direct relationship to one another and are of equal importance. Here is a compound sentence that *does not* do what it is supposed to do.

Incorrect: Theo hit the ball, <u>and</u> his mother is a nurse.

What does hitting a ball have to do with his mother being a nurse?

Now, let me throw you a curve (pun intended). Be careful. I'm out to trick you.

Theo hit the ball and ran to first base.

Where does the comma go in the above sentence? The answer is that it doesn't go anywhere. Why not? Let's examine the sentence closely. The word and does not function as a piece of cement connecting two clauses. The first part of the sentence is, indeed, a clause: [Theo hit the ball]. It contains a subject and a verb. It has a sense of completeness. The second part of the sentence does not contain a subject; [ran to first base] is not an independent clause. Listen to it aloud. Does the phrase [ran to first base] have a sense of completeness? No, it does not. It is missing the subject. Who ran to first base? Yet the sentence is fine as written and punctuated. It takes no comma. It is a simple sentence, not a compound sentence.

If you were to fall into the trap and place a comma before the word [and] in the sentence because you thought it functioned as a coordinator, the sentence would be wrong. This is another example of a run-on sentence simply because it is punctuated incorrectly. All it needs is a period.

Incorrect: Theo hit the ball [,] and ran to first base.

Correct: Theo hit the ball and ran to first base.

Correct: Theo hit the ball, and he ran to first base.

>Compound Sentence = 1 main clause + 1 main clause
>(2 main clauses)

[**Note:** An exception to the rule: If the two simple sentences in a compound sentence are very short; that is, three words or less, the comma may be omitted. However you decide to handle these sentences, be consistent. Personally, no matter the number of words in the two sentences, I generally ignore this exception and properly insert the comma between the pair of simple sentences, especially in formal writing. In prose, especially dialogue, I might adopt the exception to the rule. This is why when referencing fiction, you will see it both ways. Again, be consistent. See note regarding subordinators, page 80.]

An exception to the rule example:

The lion roared and the hunter froze.

Formal writing example:

The lion roared, and the hunter froze.

Semicolons as coordinators: [;]

In the following sentence, the semicolon takes the place of the coordinator.

Correct: Theo hit the ball; he ran to first base.

Let's go for a drive together during the wee hours. Think of a semicolon as a sort of traffic sign; it serves as a weak period in connecting clauses. It is two o'clock in the morning; there is no traffic at that hour in your neighborhood. Up ahead is a stop sign. Do *you* really come to a complete stop before continuing, or do you slow down to a virtual stop, then proceed with caution? A complete stop would be a period. Coming to a virtual stop before continuing is tantamount to employing a semicolon. When you wish to give emphasis or make an abrupt point, a semicolon can accomplish exactly that end. Let's examine the following two sentences and see how they compare with and without the use of a semicolon.

Correct: Sylvia Flynn shot her abusive husband five times, for she couldn't take any more beatings.

Correct: Sylvia Flynn shot her abusive husband five times; she couldn't take any more beatings.

By removing the coordinator [for] in the second sentence and replacing it with a semicolon, we have given a bit of pizzazz to this true account. I wrote this woman's tragic story in novel form, titled *Battered,* as she sat in prison. Read the above two sentences aloud for the full effect. Feel the punch in the latter sentence?

As the coordinating conjunction [for] functions as a substitute for another conjunction [because], let's see how we handle this piece of cement that will join the two clauses.

Correct: [Sylvia Flynn shot her abusive husband five times] because [she couldn't take any more beatings.]

You might be asking yourself why I didn't list the word because along with the other seven coordinators: and, or, but, nor, for, so and yet. The answer is that the word because, serving as cement, does not take a comma. It is the exception to the rule, yet you will see writers violate this precept out of sheer ignorance. Ignorance is simply the state of not knowing; therefore, make it your business to learn and follow these basic rules. Again, carelessness is inexcusable. In short order, the instructions I present here will clear away the cobwebs and make perfect sense as we proceed.

Now, let's see how the word because changes from a coordinator (cement) joining two clauses to beginning a sentence as a subordinator. Again, do not be intimidated with grammar terminology, for you do not have to remember this pedantic prattle because we shall continue to use less terrorizing terms as we move forward. We may simply refer to subordinators (road hazards) as danger words, words that can create a risk if not handled properly. You will see exactly why in just a moment.

So, coordinating conjunctions are nothing more than eight pieces of cement (seven of which take a comma before them and one that does not) that bond clauses. Subordinators are nothing more than danger words or road hazards. Let's go down that road together right now.

Read the following phrase aloud.

Incorrect: Because you are making an investment in time.

Does the above phrase have a sense of completeness? No, it does not.
Read the following sentence aloud.

Correct: You are making an investment in time.

Do the words above have a sense of completeness? Yes, they do.

[Because you are making an investment in time.] is a clause that has no sense of completeness. It needs an independent clause to complete it. Because I placed the word [Because] at the beginning of this sentence, I created a fragment. Let's make this into a complete sentence.

Because Russ is making an investment in time he is going to come out a winner.

We now have a complete sentence; however, we have a problem with punctuation. We must separate the two parts (clauses) with a comma. Before giving you the rule in order to do this, can you sense where the comma goes? Read the sentence aloud and *feel* the pause. That is precisely where you place your comma.

Because Russ is making an investment in time[,] he is going to come out a winner.

You have just tackled a <u>complex sentence</u>. Now, for the rule:

Complex Sentence = 1 subordinate clause (or more) + 1 main clause. We are going to keep things simple by keeping to 1 subordinate clause + 1 main clause.

The <u>subordinate clause</u>, beginning with the danger word [Because] (which would otherwise lead you to commit a fragment if you did not complete the sentence with a main clause) is as follows.

Fragment: [Because Russ is making an investment in time]

Following the subordinate clause, the main clause is going to be [he is going to come out a winner.]

1 subordinate clause + 1 main clause

[Because Russ is making an investment in time], [he is going to come out a winner.]

Don't forget the comma, which separates the subordinate clause from the main clause.

Correct: Because Russ is making an investment in time, he is going to come out a winner.

Here is a short list of common <u>subordinators</u> (danger words) that begin a sentence: After, Although, As, Because, Before, If, Since, Unless, Until — et cetera. Let's see how a few of these potentially troublesome danger words are employed.

after
although
as
because
before
if
since
unless
until

After Russ completes this course, he will be on his way to fine writing.

Although Russ may be new at this game, he will succeed.

As this is the seventh lesson, it is time to introduce a bit of 'need-to-know' grammar.

Before Russ can achieve his goal, he will have to chip away at these lessons.

If Russ can do this, he will be a winner.

Depending on its placement in a sentence, the word because is used as either a subordinator or a coordinator. Remember, if the word because begins the sentence, it is a subordinator. If the word because separates two main clauses, because is a coordinator that is not preceded by a comma.

[**Note:** Similarly, as with coordination, the exception to the rule regarding subordination is that if the dependent clause (subordinate clause) is three words or less, the comma may be omitted. However you decide to handle these sentences, be consistent. Personally, no matter the number of words beginning the subordinate clause, I generally ignore this exception to the rule in a complex sentence and properly insert the comma between the dependent (subordinate) and independent (main) clauses, especially in formal writing. In prose, especially dialogue, I might adopt the exception to the rule. Again, this is why when referencing fiction, you will see it both ways. Be consistent.]

An exception to the rule example:

As the lion roared the hunter froze.

Formal writing example:

As the lion roared, the hunter froze.

We have just covered three types of sentences, which can be handled in different ways.

Simple Sentence = 1 main clause
Compound Sentence = 2 main clauses
Complex Sentence = 1 subordinate clause + 1 main clause

Let's abbreviate the above:
SS = 1 MC
CP = 2 MCs
CPLX = 1 SUB + 1MC

Keep in mind, too, that a sentence is a grammatical unit containing one or more words that must have a sense of completeness, be it a declarative statement, a request, a question, or a command. For example, the single verb Go is a perfectly good sentence. Ah, but you might be asking, "Where is the subject in this single word sentence?" The answer is that the subject is implied. If I look *you* in the eyes and say to *you*, "Go," the undeclared subject is *you*.

Let's go back to Theo in my novel *The Teacher*.

Employing the word **then** in your prose:

The adverb **then** connecting clauses in a sentence is fraught with confusion. Much like the Oxford (or serial) Comma discussed in Lesson 4, the adverb **then** boils down to a stylistic choice. Some editors would place a comma before it, some would not. In my novel *The Teacher*, the editor/publisher wanted the comma before the adverb **then** as shown in the first example, whereas I wrote the sentence without the comma as indicated in the second example:

Theo set aside the file [,] then pulled a stack of papers in front of him.
Theo set aside the file then pulled a stack of papers in front of him.

Avoid these inaccurate forms:

Theo set aside the file and pulled a stack of papers in front of him.

Unless Theo were doing the two actions at the same time, and is employed unsoundly here because it was not (at least in my mind's eye) a simultaneous action.

Theo set aside the file and then pulled a stack of papers in front of him.

and then is doubly troublesome because of its repetitiveness as well as Theo having performed two distinct actions.

You could, of course, rework the sentence to make it quite clear:

First, Theo set aside the file; next, he pulled a stack of papers in front of him.

In the above example, two separate actions are clearly presented. We'll get into punctuating this more sophisticated type of sentence later. In the meantime, do not confuse the two sound-alike words **then** and **than**.

then (meaning at that time)
Theo flew to the crime scene on Shelter Island, but **then** he was driven home.

than (used to compare unlike things)
Theo's fish was far bigger **than** mine.

Whether (not weather) you realize it or not, we have covered a lot (not alot) of ground. Slowly and carefully, we are eradicating many errors that plague writers.

Let's move on to an even more complex type of sentence, appropriately named the compound-complex. A compound-complex sentence is a sentence having 1 (or more) subordinate clauses + 2 (or more) main clauses. So that we do not make this lesson too *complex*, we will not go beyond the 1 subordinate clause + 2 main clauses.

Compound-Complex Sentence = 1 subordinate clause + 1 main clause + 1 main clause
(that is, 1 subordinate clause + 2 main clauses)
(1 Sub + 2 MCs)

[1 subordinate clause] + [1 main clauses] + [1 main clause]

[Since you have already put in a good amount of time studying grammar,] [it would prove imprudent for you to quit,] [so hang in there.]

Don't forget to cement the subordinate clause to the main clause with a comma. Don't forget to cement the two main clauses with a comma, too.

Correct: Since you have already put in a good amount of time studying grammar, it would prove imprudent for you to quit, so hang in there.

Let's examine the same compound-complex sentence but punctuated differently.

Correct: Since you have already put in a good amount of time studying grammar, it would prove imprudent for you to quit; hang in there.

Remember, the semicolon takes the place of the comma as well as the coordinator (cement) so.

If we do not learn how to combine sentences by employing proper coordination and subordination, we would have to resort to writing a string of single, boring, choppy sentences.

Example: You have already put in a good amount of time studying grammar. It would prove imprudent for you to quit. Hang in there.

I'm sure you will agree that the three sentences formed above are, indeed, a bit choppy, unlike the compound, complex, and compound-complex sentences that incorporated proper punctuation. That is why learning to combine sentences is important to good writing.

In the next lesson, we will examine a more sophisticated form of sentence structure. Once you master it, intermingled among the four types of sentences we have covered thus far (simple sentence, compound sentence, complex sentence, compound-complex sentence) you will have the utmost confidence in setting down sentence after sentence, paragraph after paragraph. Organizing those paragraphs to their maximum advantage will be one of your final lessons. After that, you will be able to handle a number of writing projects, anything from a business letter to a tome.

First, I would like you to familiarize yourself with a number of [adverbial conjunctions](). Once more, do not be intimidated by these grammar terms: coordinating conjunctions, subordinating conjunctions, and adverbial conjunctions. As before, less offensive wording (euphemisms) will be used to label such seemingly scary mouthfuls of mumbo jumbo. If we pause to examine the term [adverbial conjunction](), we begin to see that it is part adverb and part conjunction. If we stop to analyze the term, it might actually make sense. Let's take but a moment to do exactly that.

An adverb modifies a verb, an adjective, or another adverb. That's a simple dictionary definition. But what does that mean, it modifies? It means that it *changes* the form of a verb, adjective, or another adverb. Modify means to change. So why didn't my grammar school teachers simply say that? Why was it that when I finally had a clue as to what English teachers were talking about in a New Jersey elementary school did they refer to an adverbial conjunction as a conjunctive adverb in the New York school to which I was transferred? Were all these teachers fundamentally frustrated folk who flunked out of law school yet wished to flaunt an arcane language in front of a flock of bewildered fledglings? I was not alone! In the middle of one lesson, I leaned over and asked a bright-looking girl if she had any idea of what the teacher was talking about. She shrugged her shoulders, shook her head, and asked me if I had any gum. For some reason, that was a defining moment in my life.

****

Before finishing this lesson, let's clear up a few questions that tend to befuddle new writers—maybe not so new. Those questions are usually questions about questions. Cute, I know.

Rhetorical and Tag Questions

So that we are on the same page, let's define a [rhetorical question](). A rhetorical question is a question asked when an answer is not really expected. It is being asked for effect, not for an intended reply.

A problem that plagues many writers of both fiction and nonfiction is whether or not a question mark is needed when writing a rhetorical question. The answer is, generally, yes. However, when employing *dialogue*, a rhetorical question can simply end in a period; the choice is yours. I choose not to end dialogue questions with a period. Instead, I'll employ either a question mark (?) or an exclamation point (!) Note how the two punctuation marks are employed.

Is the Pope Catholic?
Are you positively crazy!

A tag question is an inquiry that terminates with an actual question after first stating what is believed to be so and therefore needs a question mark.

Correct: She is famished, isn't she?

In formal writing, it is incorrect to combine punctuation marks. For example:

Incorrect: Are you positively crazy?!

Correct: Are you positively crazy!
    Correct: Are you positively crazy?

Referencing the above, you may come across the word interrobang. An interrobang is an obscure punctuation mark superimposing an exclamation point upon a question mark. In a word, *fugetaboutit*! You don't need or want it.

It is more important that you understand general grammar rules when engaging certain types of rhetorical questions. Here is one such example that does not need a question mark because it is a polite request.

Correct: Would all passengers please report to the check-in area.

Rhetorical questions that are presented in the form of a polite request generally do not take or need a question mark.

Sentence Tag

Correct: I shot my husband in cold blood, not realizing that his brother saw me.

The phrase not realizing that his brother saw me is an afterthought, referred to as a tag. Be sure to insert a comma between the main clause and the tag.

LESSON 8

Continued Contextual, Grammatical and Syntactical Problems that Plague Writers ~ Part II

Taking a breather from lessons in grammar and spelling is absolutely essential so that students will not become bogged down with what would otherwise be quite boring material. Pacing yourself is the key. Don't push ahead if you haven't absorbed each lesson up to this point. Again, take it nice and slow. By substituting the more easily understood and less offensive language of euphemisms rather than continuously using intimidating grammar terminology, students can *begin* to grasp the method to this otherwise convoluted code. I use the word *begin* altogether carefully, for perhaps it hasn't quite dawned on some folks as to how these grammar terms actually function. Perhaps you truly don't care. I can't say that I blame you. You'll remember how intimidated *I* felt trying to decipher rhyme or reason from a pedantic lexicon. Nonetheless, I'm going to ask that you spend a moment to note the seemingly lofty language—which often leads to sheer (not shear) confusion—juxtaposed alongside the clarity of a more down-to-earth unpretentious approach. The result will prove illuminating. Allow the following to stand as a review as well as shedding new light to help clarify what might otherwise remain obscure.

Let's examine the word *simple*: easy to understand. A simple sentence has a clause that contains a subject-verb unit.

Example: John Flynn abused his wife.
The verb is *abused*. *John Flynn* is the subject.

Pretty simple. Yes?

Let's examine the definition of the word *compound*: composed of two or more parts. That's pretty straightforward; a compound sentence is composed of two parts, connected with a piece of cement—a coordinating conjunction.

A *coordinate* (noun form, pronounced ko·ôr·dn·it) is something of equal rank.
A *conjunction* is a connection.

Therefore, grammatically speaking, a compound sentence is composed of two parts (two simple sentences), equal in rank (meaning that they are related to one another) and connected to one another by a coordinator (*and, or, but, nor, for, so, yet*);

that is, coordinating conjunctions, which I euphemistically refer to as cement, glue, et cetera.

Correct: John Flynn physically abused his wife, and he hit other people.

Two simple sentences (main clauses; also referred to as independent clauses) connected by one of the seven pieces of cement (*and, or, but, nor, for, so, yet*).

Next, let's examine the definition of the word *complex*: hard to understand. A complex sentence has one or more dependent (subordinate) clauses; in other words, they cannot stand independently as a sentence. In addition to one or more dependent (subordinate) clauses, a complex sentence has an independent (main) clause. First, let's view the dependent clause beginning with the (danger) word *Whenever*.

Incorrect: Whenever John Flynn abused his wife.

If we were to leave the phrase stand as such, it would be fragmented (incomplete). It leaves us hanging. Whenever John Flynn abused his wife, what happened? The phrase is dependent on the main clause in order to give the sentence a sense of completeness. The dependent clause [Whenever John Flynn physically abused his wife] is subordinate to the independent clause [she cringed.] In other words, the dependent clause is lower in rank; it cannot stand by itself. [Whenever John Flynn physically abused his wife, she cringed.] Again, the dependent clause (subordinate clause) is connected to the independent (main) clause by an important piece of punctuation; specifically, the comma you see between *wife* and *she*. The danger word (subordinator) [Whenever] appearing as the first word, signals us that punctuation is needed.

Correct: Whenever John Flynn physically abused his wife, she cringed.

This is becoming a bit more complex. Yes? But defining these terms grammatically helps us to understand what might otherwise remain an arcane language. To apply the rules is one thing; to have a basic comprehension of the lingo attached to the rules will serve to reinforce these lessons.

Are you ready for more abuse?

The compound-complex sentence is compounded by the fact that the lesson is becoming more complex. The compound-complex sentence has one or more dependent (subordinate) clauses and two or more coordinate [equal in rank] independent (main) clauses. In the next example, we'll examine the sentence containing one dependent (subordinate) clause and two independent (main) clauses. Be reminded that the dependent (subordinate) clause is connected to the independent (main) clause by a comma. Also, bear in mind that the two independent (main) clauses are connected with a coordinating conjunction (cement = *and, or, but, nor, for, so, yet*), preceded by a comma.

```
        [subordinate clause]                    [main clause] [conj.]
[Whenever John Flynn physically abused his wife,] [she cringed,] [for] [Sylvia
        [main clause]
knew that one day he would kill her.]
```

Correct: Whenever John Flynn physically abused his wife, she cringed, for Sylvia knew that one day he would kill her.

To continue our lessons in sentence structure, let's examine a more sophisticatedly constructed sentence; a sentence with an adverbial conjunction [however] placed between two independent (main) clauses, preceded by a dependent (subordinate) clause.

```
        [subordinate clause]                    [main clause] [adv. conj.]
[Whenever John Flynn physically abused his wife,] [she cringed;] [however,]
        [main clause]
[one day the woman retaliated.]
```

[Whenever John Flynn physically abused his wife] [,] she cringed [;] [however] [,] [one day the woman retaliated.]

Whenever John Flynn physically abused his wife, she cringed; however, one day the woman retaliated.

Once again, nice and clean.

Correct: Whenever John Flynn physically abused his wife, she cringed; however, one day the woman retaliated.

If you have these lessons placed solidly under your thinking cap (especially this last sentence with the adverbial conjunction placed in the middle of it), you are to be congratulated; furthermore, you will be rewarded.

We have covered simple sentences, run-ons and fragments, commas and semicolons, coordinators and coordinating conjunctions; subordinators and subordinating conjunctions, compound and complex sentences, compound-complex sentences, independent and dependent clauses, adverbs and adverbial conjunctions.

What a mixed bag of mumbo jumbo. I trust that some light has been shed upon this confusion and that you are on your way to proceeding with confidence. Recognizing danger curves as we continue en route, along with knowing when and how to apply the brakes (not breaks), will help you reach the end of this journey with your sanity intact.

Restrictive and Nonrestrictive Clauses

Before we move ahead, let's examine still another form of subordination so that you will have total confidence in determining whether or not commas are to be used to offset parenthetical information in a particular sentence. The grammatical terms that refer to these types of sentences are <u>restrictive</u> and <u>nonrestrictive</u> clauses. To decide which is which, you'll merely ask yourself whether or not the clause is necessary or unnecessary for a fundamental identification of the subject. If the clause is unnecessary for identifying the subject, commas are needed because the identification is parenthetical and would not restrict the subject's ID if the clause were removed. Example:

specific
subject
Correct: [Donald], who became president of the United States, won the Electoral College vote.

Note that the subordinate clause is parenthetical (added) information because we already have a specific subject; that is, [Donald]. Therefore, the parenthetical phrase needs to be offset with commas.

If the subject is not specific, the subordinate clause is, indeed, necessary for identifying the subject; that is, [The man]. Hence, commas are not needed because it would otherwise restrict the subject's ID. Example:

nonspecific
subject
Correct: [The man] who became president of the United States won the Electoral College vote.

You may be thinking: *Yeah, but doesn't the fact that* [The man] *won the Electoral College vote necessarily point to Donald Trump?*

No, it does not because four other presidents lost the popular vote but won the electoral vote: John Quincy Adams, Rutherford B. Hayes, Benjamin Harrison, and George W. Bush. Donald J. Trump makes five.

Let's present other examples in order to reinforce this important lesson.

nonspecific
subject
Correct: [The author's novel] which was originally published in 1991 was later republished under a different title.

Incorrect: [The author's novel], which was originally published in 1991, was later republished under a different title.

      specific
      subject
Correct: [Bob's novel], which was originally published in 1991, was later republished under a different title.

      specific
      subject
Incorrect: [Markus] who loves to fish moved to Florida.

Correct: [Markus], who loves to fish, moved to Florida.

      nonspecific
      subject
Incorrect: [The man], who loves to fish, moved to Florida.

Correct: [The man] who loves to fish moved to Florida.

Note, too, that *who* refers to people and *which* refers to things as well as places.

    In the previous chapter, we left off observing several adverbs, about to place and shape them into rather sophisticated sentence structure. Among the four basic types of sentences are the simple, compound, complex, and compound-complex forms—along with variations thereof (sentences that you now have under your belt). You are about to construct a rather intricate form. It is an elaborate sentence to add to your arsenal. You might consider it your heaviest piece of artillery. But first a quick review.

    You now know how to handle <u>cement</u> (coordinators and coordinating conjunctions):

                          and
                          or
                          but
                          nor
                          for
                          so
                          yet
        because [as a coordinator ~ no comma before it]

    You are also aware of <u>danger or hazard words</u> (subordinators and subordinating conjunctions). Again, here are a few examples:

> after
> although
> as
> because
> if
> since
> unless
> until
>
> because [as a subordinator beginning a sentence]

Now, let's take a look at a handful of adverbial conjunctions, which we'll employ in our sophisticated-styled sentences. What less offensive term could we apply to them? How about form changers? As good as any, I imagine. Here is but a smattering:

> consequently
> furthermore
> however
> moreover
> nonetheless
> nevertheless
> therefore
> inasmuch as
> insofar as

[**Note:** The last two items on the list may be referred to as adverbial phrases because they consist of more than one word; therefore, don't let it throw you.]

Observe carefully how my preceding sentence is constructed:

[1st main clause]
[The last two items on the list may be referred to as adverbial phrases because they consist of more than one word]; therefore, [don't let it throw you.]
[adv. conj.]   [2nd main clause]

Note that the sentence has the adverbial conjunction therefore placed between the two main clauses.

The magic is to place a semicolon immediately after the first main clause. Why? The answer is that the semicolon serves as a weak period, allowing you to continue the sentence. Because it is not a true period, you do not capitalize the adverbial conjunction [therefore]. Immediately following the conjunction [therefore], you place a comma in order to connect it to the second main clause. Hence, we have properly constructed and punctuated a rather sophisticated sentence with an adverbial conjunction tucked between two main clauses.

Incorrect: The last two items on the list may be referred to as adverbial phrases because they consist of more than one word; Therefore, don't let it throw you.

Correct: The last two items on the list may be referred to as adverbial phrases because they consist of more than one word; therefore, don't let it throw you.

Also, we could make this sentence into two sentences.

Correct: The last two items on the list may be referred to as adverbial phrases because they consist of more than one word. Therefore, don't let it throw you.

Let's examine another sentence using a different adverbial conjunction (form changer) tucked between two main clauses. Let's examine the adverbial conjunction [however].

I can't believe that I'm finally beginning to understand the basics and beyond; however, I am going to remain cautiously optimistic.

The sophisticated sentence employing an adverbial conjunction = 1 main clause + an adverbial conjunction + 1 main clause.

However, it's time to throw you another curve. I know, just when you were getting into the swing of things.

Let's stay with the conjunction [however] and note its form change. Below, we have the adverb tucked away in a sentence; however, we do not treat it as an adverbial conjunction because it is not connecting two main clauses. It is simply an adverb that separates the clause. When instructing in the classroom, rather animatedly, I stand on a chair and, in a normal voice, say I will—then I immediately get off the chair, drop my voice, practically whispering the word however—immediately get back up on the chair and say, endeavor to keep up. Punctuated correctly, it looks and reads like this:

I will, however, endeavor to keep up.

Do this in the privacy of your home (not at a dinner party). Say it aloud, and you will *feel* the pause, which necessitates placing commas on each side of the adverbial conjunction however.

Correct: I will, however, endeavor to keep up.

Incorrect: I will; however, endeavor to keep up.

Incorrect: I will, however; endeavor to keep up.

In the next sophisticated sentence form, we'll begin with a <u>subordinate clause</u> (phrase), followed by a <u>main clause,</u> then employ however as an <u>adverbial conjunction,</u> and finally conclude with a second main clause. Keep in mind that everything is easy once you know how. Ready?

[1 subordinate clause]   [1ˢᵗ main clause]   [advb. conj.]
[As we were walking through the park,] [I found a five dollar bill;] [however,]
    [2ⁿᵈ main clause]
[Russ snatched it from my hand.]

Correct: As we were walking through the park, I found a five dollar bill; however, Russ snatched it from my hand.

The key will now be to use a variety of sentence structure in *your* writing. Just don't use one or two types of sentences. Use them all. Once you feel confident, sentence-wise, you will be ready to tackle paragraph after paragraph, moving on to the organization of those paragraphs, which we'll cover in the next chapter.

Understanding how grammarians came up with terms that obfuscate rather than illuminate will prove helpful in deciphering future encounters with apparent forms of seemingly covert code. Hence, we find the pedant at his or her best . . . or worst. Here we will connect literal terminology to the applied grammar terms so as to make some sense of them. Take this nice and slow, and don't let it throw you. Try and digest the often complicated path grammarians have set for us.

Coordinating conjunction:
coordinating: working together harmoniously; equal, especially in rank
conjunction: conjoining; a joining together

Grammar-wise, we have two parts of a sentence (main clauses) joined together with <u>cement</u> (coordinating conjunction), preceded by a comma.

To complicate matters, those main clauses may also be referred to as independent clauses because they can stand alone.

Subordinating conjunction:
subordinating: placed in a lower rank or class
conjunction: conjoining; a joining together

Grammar-wise, we have one part of a sentence (subordinate clause) joined to another (main clause) separated by a comma.

To complicate matters, the one clause (subordinate clause) may also be referred to as a dependent clause because it cannot stand alone.

Adverbial conjunction:
adverbial   functions as a modifier; form changer
conjunction   conjoining; a joining together

Grammar-wise, we have one part of a sentence set as a main clause, joined to a second part of the sentence with an adverbial conjunction (subordinate in rank), preceded by a semicolon—followed by a comma, then joined to a third part of the sentence with another main clause.

To further complicate matters, the phrase beginning with an adverbial conjunction (subordinate part) may also be referred to as a dependent clause because it cannot stand alone.

Conversely, we have a fairly good sense in understanding the terminology put forth by grammarians as applied to our four basic types of sentences: simple, compound, complex, compound-complex. It's pretty much straightforward. For example, let's take the compound sentence.

Compound sentence:
compound: composed of two or more parts, elements, ingredients
sentence: a grammatical unit

Grammar-wise, we have two units joined together by (we're coming full circle, here) a coordinating conjunction, and it is at this juncture that grammarians become heavy handed with their language. Labeling the term 'cement' or 'glue' in lieu of coordinating conjunctions is not only less intimidating than that eight-syllable phrase, it immediately creates a picture in your mind as to what a coordinating conjunction is intended to do.

To complicate matters beyond the four basic types of sentences as well as more intricate sentences formed with adverbial conjunctions tucked away between clauses, be they main clauses or subordinate clauses (synonymous with independent and dependent clauses, respectively), grammarians have ironically created a greater complexity in structuring their own language; that is, a jargon supposedly employed to elucidate the subject—not complicate it.

Keep in mind that sentences do many different things. They may make statements, give commands, instruct, advise, or make requests, ask questions, convey strong feelings or emotions. These sentences fall into four basic categories:

Sentences that make a statement (your most common type) are called **declarative sentences**.

Sentences that give commands, instructions, advice, or make requests are called **imperative sentences**.

Sentences that ask questions are called **interrogative sentences**.

Sentences that convey strong feelings or emotions are called **exclamatory sentences**.

The following sentences are examples of each type.

declarative sentence ~ I'm going to make him an offer he can't refuse.[statement]
imperative sentence ~ I demand that you digest these grammar lessons in small doses. [command]
imperative sentence ~ Study these grammar lessons for approximately thirty minutes at a clip. [instruction]
imperative sentence ~ It's wiser to work smarter than harder. [advice]
imperative sentence ~ Please devote thirty minutes a day, every day, to your grammar studies. [request]
interrogative sentence ~ Do you think you can do this for yourself? [question]
exclamatory sentence ~ I hate editing! [strong feeling or emotion]
exclamatory sentence ~ I love writing! [strong feeling or emotion]

Prepositions

A preposition is a word that precedes a noun or a pronoun to show a relationship to another word in the sentence.

Common prepositions:

about, across, against, along, among, around, at, before, behind, below, beneath, beside, between, beyond, by, down, during, except, for, from, in, inside, into, like, near, of, off, on, since, to, toward, through, under, until, up, upon, with, within.

Crime thrillers *about* serial killers intrigue many readers.

The preposition *about* shows the relationship between thrillers and serial killers.

A prepositional phrase (more than one word) shows a relationship to another word in the sentence.

Crime thrillers *about serial killers* intrigue many readers.

The prepositional phrase is *about serial killers* and shows a relationship to thrillers.

Personal Pronouns that Plague Writers

SINGULAR	Subjective pronoun	Objective pronoun	Possessive pronouns	Possessive modifier
First Person	I	me	mine	my
Second person	you	you	yours	your
Third Person	he	him	his	his
	she	her	hers	her
	it	it	its	its
PLURAL				
First Person	we	us	ours	our
Second person	you	you	yours	your
Third Person	they	them	theirs	their

When deciding on the correct pronoun, rely on your ears as to which form is correct.

Example: Donna and *I/me* love fishing.

Now, simply remove Donna from the sentence, and rely on your ears as to which form sounds correct.

Incorrect: *Me* love fishing.

Correct: *I* love fishing.

Correct Full Sentence: Donna and I love fishing.

Let's deal with a trickier sentence.

Example: Let Tim and *I/me* do the introductions.

Now, simply remove Tim from the sentence, and, again, rely on your ears as to which form sounds correct.

Incorrect: Let *I* do the introductions.

Correct: Let *me* do the introductions.

Correct Full Sentence: Let Tim and me do the introductions.

Whereas you relied on your ears in deciding which pronoun to use correctly, the following is a rule that you will just have to remember: When writing the phrase Between you and I/me, always use the pronoun *me*; never use Between you and *I*.

Example: Between you and *I/me,* John believes that President Trump is going to turn this country around for the better.

Correct: Between you and *me,* John believes that President Trump is going to turn this country around for the better.

Incorrect: Between you and *I,* John believes that President Trump is going to turn this country around for the better.

Who versus Whom

Here are two troublesome <u>pronouns</u> that plague many writers and speakers alike. When to use **Who** and **Whom**. Once again, your ears are often your best grammar tools; however, you need to know the rules as well in order to be certain.

Rather than depend solely on our ears as grammar tools, let's apply the rules concerning **who** and **whom**.

Who is always used as the <u>subject</u> of a sentence or clause.
Whom is always used as the <u>object</u> of a sentence or clause.

| I | you | he | she | it | we | they ~ are <u>subject</u> pronouns |
| me | you | him | her | it | us | them ~ are <u>object</u> pronouns |

Which of the following sentences is correct?

For **who** should I vote?
For **whom** should I vote?

First, simply ask yourself: For which candidate should I vote?

Next, answer yourself:

Should I vote for **him**?
Should I vote for **her**?
Should I vote for **he**?
Should I vote for **she**?

I	you	he	she	it	we	they	~ are subject pronouns = who
me	you	him	her	it	us	them	~ are object pronouns = whom

him and her are object pronouns; therefore, whom is the correct.

Correct: For whom should I vote?
Incorrect: For who should I vote?

Which of the following two sentences is correct?

Whom wrote the letter?
Who wrote the letter?

Let's examine these seven correct subject pronouns:
I wrote the letter.
You wrote the letter.
He wrote the letter.
She wrote the letter.
It wrote the letter.
We wrote the letter.
They wrote the letter.

Five of these seven object pronouns are incorrect; two are correct.
Me wrote the letter.
You wrote the letter.
Him wrote the letter.
Her wrote the letter.
It wrote the letter.
Us wrote the letter.
Them wrote the letter.

Note that You and It can serve as both subject pronouns and object pronouns.

If you're having trouble comprehending the sentence [It wrote the letter], it could mean that perhaps a monster wrote the letter.

Whom wrote the letter sounds incorrect, and it is.
Who wrote the letter sounds correct, and it is.

Correct: Who wrote the letter?
Incorrect: Whom wrote the letter?

Once again for reinforcement:

I   you   he   she   it   we   they ~ are <u>subject</u> pronouns = who
me   you   him   her   it   us   them ~ are <u>object</u> pronouns = whom

Which of the following sentences is correct?

Two men stood before the fountain, one of **who** had blond hair and blue eyes.
Two men stood before the fountain, one of **whom** had blond hair and blue eyes.

Incorrect: Two men stood before the fountain, one of **who** had blond hair and blue eyes.

Correct: Two men stood before the fountain, one of **whom** had blond hair and blue eyes.

Why is the second sentence correct?

If **they** takes the <u>subject</u> pronoun **who**, the prepositional phrase (of who) would read: one of they had blond hair and blue eyes.

If **them** takes the <u>object</u> pronoun **whom**, the prepositional phrase (of whom) would read: one of **them** had blond hair and blue eyes.

And once again for reinforcement:

I   you   he   she   it   we   they ~ are <u>subject</u> pronouns = who
me   you   him   her   it   us   them ~ are <u>object</u> pronouns = whom

Of course, you could take the lazy way out and simply avoid using **who** or **whom** altogether.

Correct: Two men stood before the fountain. One man had blond hair and blue eyes.
or
Correct: Two men stood before the fountain; one of the men had blond hair and blue eyes.

However, I want you to have several options available in your arsenal for handling such sentences, along with the confidence that you are employing those choices correctly.

That versus Which

The rule: If the sentence doesn't need the clause that the word in question is connecting, use *which*. If it does, use *that*. Here is an example.

Our office, which has two lunchrooms, is located in Cincinnati.
Our office that has two lunchrooms is located in Cincinnati.

These two sentences do not mean the same. The first sentence is saying that there is one office and that it in Cincinnati. The phrase *which has two lunchrooms* gives additional information, but it doesn't change the meaning of the sentence. Remove the phrase and the location of the office would still be clear: Our office is located in Cincinnati.

The second sentence suggests that there is more than one office, but *the office with two lunchrooms* is in Cincinnati. The phrase *that has two lunchrooms* is known as a restrictive clause because another part of the sentence, the office, depends on it. Removing that phrase changes the meaning of the sentence.

Well, that's enough grammar and grammar talk for the moment. In the next lesson, we'll shift gears and examine something a bit more appealing: **Book Titles and Cover Designs**.

LESSON 9

Book Titles and Cover Designs

Titles, especially heading short fictional pieces such as Shirley Jackson's *The Lottery*, could and, perhaps, should be a bit . . . ambiguous. Remember how you were initially duped when comparing the title to the beginning and ending of the story? However, nothing is written in stone, except Irving. Get it? Irving Stone, the prolific biographical novelist of Michelangelo's *The Agony and the Ecstasy*. I know. Bad joke. But I exampled that particular title because the two nouns (agony and ecstasy) are somewhat apropos to the writing process in general: The *agony* of writing and the *ecstasy* of having written. Actually, it is not a very good comparison because Stone's story has nothing to do with the writing process. I was initially thinking out loud. Take the time to think . . . a bit longer. . . . Yet, in a sense, Michelangelo's artistic struggle between his skillful sculpting ability and questioning mural-painting adequacy to please the pope is certainly analogous; hence, the *agony*. The finished fresco, however, upon the ceiling in the Sistine Chapel is, of course, the artist's *ecstasy*. A better example might be to quote short story writer Dorothy Parker. "I hate writing; I love having written." It's that very struggle to achieve a beginning, middle, and an end that can take its toll, coupled to the rules of grammar. Ah, but once having arrived at that point, love exudes through every pore of your being.

Apart from the Shirley Jackson example (*The Lottery*) cited above, titles for most any written work should capture and convey its pure essence. A good title does more than hint; it generally reveals. Coupled to the title, be it a work of fiction or nonfiction, a depiction denoting the subject matter upon the book's cover certainly helps to achieve this end. Conversely, a title or book's illustration that conveys no such message must then rely solely on the author's established known classification (genre) of repute: murder mystery, historical romance, horror, westerns, et cetera. Be smart and choose your titles and cover designs most carefully. It would be a shame to have good book compromised by a poor title and/or cover design.

Case in point: The cover of my first novel titled *No Stranger Than I* (later republished as *Dicky, Richard, and I*), beheld a black and white photograph of the nebula Trifed, which served, in my mind's eye, as a representation of the human brain —a perfect pictorial metaphor. When I presented the photograph and the negative to the graphics people at the publishing house, the image was crystal clear; however, when the photo was reproduced as a cover for the book, it was a bit blurry. Unfortunately, it was too late for me to do anything about it. I had proofread the galley sheets; I had never seen the cover until after two thousand copies of the book had been printed. Shame on me. I had more than a couple of folks tell me that when they browsed their bookstores and spotted the book, folks thought it was about astronomy until they read the back cover. It is your responsibility to stay on top of everything. The new printing, *Dicky, Richard, and I*, had a far better title and cover design.

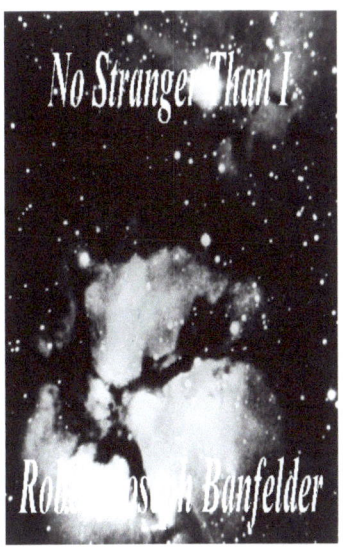 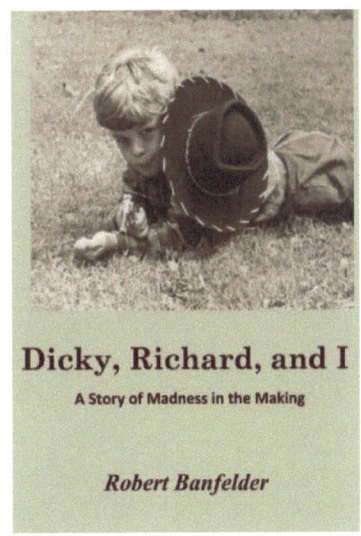

In the next lesson, titled **Organizing Paragraphs for Article Writing ~ Writing Models**, we will be reading and examining an editorial that I wrote concerning a young man who was sent to prison for a sex crime he absolutely did not commit. I went on to write an extensive series of articles on the case. The police had railroaded the man, and those in authority were allowing the charade to continue. Therefore, my titles were designed to bring attention to these facts. With the exception of the third nondescript title, let's see if they do indeed capture the essence of my intent. The authorities that comprised the lot were Queens County, New York police officials; the Queens District Attorney; one of his ADAs; the presiding judge; and the Queens Sex Crime Unit.

Police Prevarication: The Long and the Short of It
Dances with DA's
Men and Machinery
DA's Gambit: Deals, Deceptions, and Delays
ADA: Master of Duplicity or Darling of Dunces?
Justice Delayed is Justice Denied
Truth, Justice, and the American Way of Life: Guilty Until Proven Innocent
The Queens Sex Crimes Unit: Abusers of Power
The Best of Times, the Worst of Times

I'd like to quickly mention that because of perseverance on the part of several of us, the man was released from prison.

We'll examine other titles, some of which you may already be familiar with, but first an introduction.

When I was an undergraduate in a Creative Writing Program at Queens College, New York, I had a most interesting instructor, Wallace Markfield. Mr. Markfield had written a couple of novels at the time, the first of which was made into a film. The screenplay, *Bye Bye Braverman*, was adapted from the author's novel, *To An Early Grave*, an American comedy. I still have the book in the form of advance sheets, personalized and autographed by the satirist: "For Robert Banfelder—who will pay list price for the next one. With all good wishes, Wallace Markfield." And I did pay list price for his next book titled, *Teitlebaum's Window*, which Wallace also personalized and autographed: "For Robert Banfelder—who has (perhaps) also looked through that window. Wallace Markfield." Then came *You Could Live If They Let You*: "For Bob Banfelder—who has lightened these dark times. Wallace Markfield."

Through the years, Wallace, his wife Anna, along with Donna and I, had spent some quality time together. Donna and I would drive to the couple's home in Port Washington, New York, have dinner, sip wine, then listen to and critique Wallace's work while he puffed on a cigar. He appreciated our candid comments. The book we bantered about before its publication was *Radical Surgery*. Along came another personalized and autographed copy of that novel: "For Bob and Donna—who know that we live in dark times. With love. Wallace Markfield." *Radical Surgery* was Wallace's last published work, though he had another manuscript in the wings. Then it became my turn to read and have my work critiqued. 'Twas a good thing that I had a glass of wine or two to chase away the jitters. The man's advice proved invaluable.

Wallace's four titles, in and of themselves, do not necessarily reveal the nature of the work until they are coupled with the books' covers. A bit more telling. Rather than belabor the point, Google the author's name and book titles for a clearer understanding.

Wallace Markfield's novels:

To An Early Grave
Teitlebaum's Window
You Could Live If They Let You
Radical Surgery

Back to that undergraduate class with Wallace Markfield, visiting professor at Queens College. It was my second semester with the man; his third work was in manuscript form at the time. The novel was based on a Lenny Bruce character, Jules Farber. Markfield excerpted from the work in progress and, as a class, we discussed character and content. Mr. Markfield claimed that he could not drum up a good title for his latest book and offered a small reward if anyone in the class could come up with a suitable name. One student did. *You Could Live If They Let You* appeared to fit the bill. When I went into teaching, I offered students the same deal. I had a tentative title for my first novel: *Dicky, Richard, and I*, a psychological thriller detailing the metamorphosis of a young, emotionally abused and battered child into that of a multiple murderer and personality. It was a title that I believed captured the essence of the work. Literary agents and editors liked the story yet had reservations about the title, so I had my students select a new name. To keep things fair, several titles were voted on out of my presence; *No Stranger Than I* was the preferred title by a majority of the class.

My next two novels, also psychological thrillers, homed in on two groups of professionals with whom I'm familiar; namely, authors and teachers. I kept the titles simple; hence, *The Author* and its sequel, *The Teacher*. Since eight of the nine novels deal with serial killers, I, of course, paint those characters in anything but a positive light. As mentioned earlier, extensive research went into developing and presenting each antagonist—the veritable worst of the worse.

After writing about such sociopaths, day after day, it proved a pleasant change of pace to write about a world that I paint with far brighter colors, that being, the world of the great outdoors. Although words are still my medium of expression, my brushstrokes are far broader. Upon and even beyond a canvas filled with landscapes and seascapes lies a universe of wonder. One can enter that world of astonishment by simply picking up a fishing rod, messing around with boats, or foraging and hunting for food as our ancestors had. In other words, getting back to and staying in touch with nature.

Let's examine several titled articles published in various outdoor magazines for which I write. Note not only the succinct titles, which indicate what each piece is about, but also the employment of alliteration so as to subliminally lock the theme in the reader's mind.

Somersaulting Over Shad
Striper Secrets on a Fly Rod
Gardiner's to the Greenlawns: Fluke Fishing at its Finest
Peconic Porgies: For Kids Six to Sixty
Defeating the Winter Doldrums
Smoking Fish: A Shortcut to a Savory Fare

There you have a good sampling and understanding of titles applied to fiction and nonfiction works. Let's now examine the content of a short seven-paragraph piece that I wrote for a Long Island, New York publication, *Dan's Papers*. Study it carefully. With an enthusiastic interest in a given subject, along with a bit of research, *you*, too, can put together a piece for publication, picking up a few dollars in the bargain.

Greenport's Rich Maritime Heritage
Part I
A Must-Visit Village
by Bob Banfelder

With a 2000 census population of only 2,048 folks, Greenport Village streets nevertheless teem with tourists, especially during the peak summer and fall months. Its attractions flow from a myriad of surrounding activities as more than forty vineyards dot the East End of Long Island; restaurants range from fine dining to casual fare; too, shop-till-you-drop stores and boutiques abound the area. More specifically, Greenport itself is rich in maritime history. Even early spring and late fall can draw a good crowd.

A degree of research [Greenport's census], coupled to a strong alliterative phrase [teem with tourists], paints a clear introduction to the piece. Too, I take in the encompassing area [wineries, eateries and shops]. Next, I tie in the theme of the piece [Greenport's maritime events], having linked three seasons: summer, fall, and spring.

September showcases Greenport's Maritime Festival, an annual two-day weekend event preceded by a Friday evening Land and Sea cocktail party. The happening preserves an important nautical heritage. Greenport's East End Seaport Museum and Marine Foundation is the organization that hosts the Maritime Festival.

Paragraph two succinctly supports the thesis by naming the group responsible for presenting the happenings; namely, Greenport's East End Seaport Museum and Marine Foundation.

Among the many vessels featured at the festival this year was an historical Beebe-McLellan Life-Saving Surfboat, a lapstrake half-scale model of four hundred original 25-foot 4-inch long, 7-foot beam boats that were built in the Beebe Boat Shop at the foot of Ludlum Place at Rackett's Basin in Greenport. These life-saving surfboats were constructed over a thirty-nine year period; that is, between 1879 and 1918. Following stringent testing in the Atlantic Ocean, the United States Government contracted twenty surfboats for lifesaving purposes. A proven success, hundreds were employed along the eastern seaboard of both the United States and Canada. The East End Seaport Museum and Marine Foundation commissioned the construction of a replica so as to highlight but a single historical aspect of Greenport's multifaceted marine industry.

Paragraph three homes in on one of several boats exhibited at the celebration's annual event. Specifications noted at the show regarding the historical Beebe-McLellan Life-Saving Surfboat, along with expanded information found on the Internet, framed this division.

Featured, too, at the East End Seaport Museum and Marine Foundation, located at Third Street at the Ferry Dock, is an exhibit honoring famed shark hunter Captain Frank Mundus, purported to be the quintessential model for Peter Benchley's character, Captain Quint, in the 1975 box-office hit, *Jaws*. Frank's affable daughter, Pat Mundus—a board member of the East End Seaport Museum and Marine Foundation, as well as executive director of the Shelter Island Historical Society—resides in Greenport and spoke about her late father's adventures, dispelling several myths about the man and the movie.

An interview with the daughter, coupled to my experiences with the woman's father, Frank Mundus, proved fodder for the previous and following paragraph. It is amazing how one story or interview will lead to another. Never pass on an opportunity when it presents itself.

Shortly before his death on September 10, 2008, Donna (my significant other) and I had the honor of spending the last two summers with Frank Mundus. Frank and I worked book signings together, dined out and enjoyed meals at our home along with other angling friends. Additionally, I piloted an interview with his wife, Jenny, from their home in Hawaii, as well as conducting the last extensive interview with the Monster Man himself. What I can absolutely attest to is the fact that, like Captain Quint in the film (portrayed by the actor Robert Shaw), Frank Mundus was, indeed, a true character. At 83 years old, Frank had all his faculties and was the life of the party at dinners, book signing engagements, informal talks and discussions. He loved the limelight and making people laugh. He was a kidder, a prankster, a no-nonsense soul; a man who many folks say put Montauk on the map. Mundus was recognized, along with Donnie Braddick, as having caught the world's largest great white shark on a rod and reel: 3,427 pounds. Frank also harpooned and brought in a 4,500 pound great white.

The East End Seaport Museum and Marine Foundation, a nonprofit organization, was established to recognize, restore and preserve the maritime heritage of the East End of Long Island, be it boats, seamen, or buildings. One such building, the Long Beach Bar Lighthouse, situated between Orient Harbor and Gardiner's Bay, stands as a symbolic beacon, beckoning sailors for centuries to the protected waters of Peconic Bay. The lighthouse, monikered Bug Light, was restored in 1990, the year the Foundation was instituted. The organization owns and operates the working lighthouse.

Before concluding the piece, giving well-deserved kudos to The East End Seaport Museum and Marine Foundation, the paragraph lends its best support to the theme of Greenport's rich maritime history—a symbol that has stood and salutes seamen for hundreds of years.

Greenport—originally referred to as Winter Harbor, then Stirling, Greenhill, and finally renamed Greenport—is conveniently accessible by car, bus, train or ferry. A working seaport since the 18th century, incorporated in 1838, Greenport is part of Southold Township. This charming seaport village is a jewel; a gem of a small country town. A visit to Greenport, be it summer, fall, winter or spring, will enchant you. For its fall finale, the East End Seaport Museum and Marine Foundation is finishing up with a free maritime film festival on Saturday, December 19th. In this penultimate hour, come and enjoy a children's film series commencing at 11:00 a.m.; 7:00 p.m. will take us out to sea with a talk and short documentary chronicling the long friendship between Ernest Hemingway and his boat captain, Gregorio, in *The Old Man and Hemingway*.

The last paragraph links back to the first, expanding upon the village's history while inviting folks to visit through the *four* seasons, concluding with a timely announcement of an imminent fall event.

****

Most recently, I edited a nonfiction book for a client, Samuel Berlin. Sam had titled the manuscript *Abruzzo*. Abruzzo is a region in central Italy, lying along its eastern coast. However, the name Abruzzo had only appeared once in the story, a factual account of two men's journey through German-occupied France and Italy. As part of the French underground, then later as a partisan fighting the Nazis in Italy, Samuel Berlin (alias Antonio Bruno) and his companion, Pierre Francois Cavagna, fight against Fascism and Nazism. The pair is constantly being referred to as *Il Professore* and the English spy by the peasant farmers below those mountainous areas. Hence, I suggested the title *The Professor and the English Spy*. And so it is.

As Sam and Pierre traveled extensively through the mountains, freezing and starving, creating havoc with the enemy while the two wended their way toward the front lines to join the Allied forces, a simple but powerful, colorful, nondescript photograph of a portion of elevated rocky land provided the perfect setting for the book's cover, capturing the theme.

LESSON 10

Organizing Paragraphs for Article Writing

You have been working hard to build a sound foundation. Sentence structure is at the heart of that foundation; paragraphs are the building blocks which form the edifice. Each block contributes to a unified whole. In this lesson, we will be examining a three-step paragraph writing model, a five-step paragraph model, and a more sophisticated five-step paragraph model. Your three-paragraph model will contain a beginning (thesis paragraph), a middle (support paragraph), and an end (concluding paragraph).

Let's begin by defining a thesis. A thesis is simply the main idea put forth for consideration, especially a proposition to be argued. It is the central theme of your piece whether in the form of a composition, article, book, et cetera.

Three-Step Model
First Paragraph
(Thesis)

In the first three-step model, I will discuss kayaks. What will be my thesis? There are basically two types of people-power systems for propelling a kayak: the kind you paddle and the kind you pedal. I am going to take the position that the type you paddle is a better choice than the type you pedal. That's my thesis statement: the main idea, the central theme, the proposition. It now becomes my job to state the thesis somewhere in the first paragraph. Perhaps I'll talk about kayaks in general. Maybe I'll discuss their early history.

I have students new to the writing process state their thesis in the very first sentence of the very first paragraph. It's like holding the reins of a horse; *you* are in control. Don't let go of that main idea. This way, the reader of the piece knows from the onset exactly what you will be discussing as well as your position on the subject. Example of a thesis statement: <u>Paddling is a better choice than pedaling when it comes to selecting a kayak.</u>

However, the thesis could be placed in the middle of the first paragraph, or it could be presented in the last sentence of that paragraph, serving as a bridge leading into your second paragraph. If you feel that you can handle the latter approach, creating a smooth transition into your second paragraph, by all means, give it a go. The important point is that you have your thesis somewhere in that first paragraph.

Second Paragraph
(**Good** argument)

Next, it is incumbent on you to support your thesis statement in the second paragraph. You must introduce a good argument so as to give credence to your proposition. Example of good support: You might want to write about paddling as a far superior form of exercise over pedaling, especially in terms of developing upper body strength.

Third Paragraph
(**Conclusion**)

This is the paragraph where many new students of writing go awry. Most students believe that they are to summarize the entire piece. What the writer must do, in fact, is restate the thesis statement, not recapitulate all three paragraphs. However, there is a twist to the approach. You *do not* want to be repetitive, that is, saying the same words over—verbatim. So, how do we avoid this? How do we restate the thesis without being repetitive? The answer is that you *do* restate the thesis, only you do so by using different words to make the same point. Example of a conclusion: When choosing a kayak, paddle power is a smarter alternative than pedal power.

Obviously, you do not want to present one sentence paragraphs. Therefore, you need to expand each paragraph. I've already given you some insight as how to develop the first paragraph. In order for you to elaborate on the subject, you have to first know something about kayaks, or you must research the subject. This brings us to a very important point. You either write what you know about, or you study the subject carefully if not intimately.

****

Five-Step Model
First Paragraph
(**Thesis**)

Not unlike a three-step model, the first paragraph of the five-step model contains your thesis statement. Let's stay with kayaks as a subject but alter the thesis so that you can see that there are varied approaches. You will observe precisely how these building blocks (paragraphs) are arranged in order to erect the finished product (an article worthy of publication).

First off, let's assume that you have a rather limited knowledge of kayaks; therefore, research is required. Let's presuppose that you have done your homework. After studying the subject, you learn that there are basically two kinds of kayaks, commonly referred to as Sit-On-Top types and Sit-Inside types. You have also learned that for the purpose of fishing, while considering the safety factors, Sit-On-Top kayaks (SOTs) are a far better choice than what is disparagingly referred to as the acronym (SINKS); that is, Sit-Inside Kayaks. The issue of safety is a powerful persuader. Hence, I will address a new thesis. Example: When it comes to fishing and safety, Sit-On-Top kayaks are a far better choice than Sit-Inside Kayaks.

Second Paragraph
(Good argument)

In the second paragraph of this five-step model, we need to present a good argument to support the thesis. Remember, we are presenting two aspects: fishing and safety; first, fishing from a kayak. Example: Fishing from a Sit-On-Top kayak allows for unencumbered maneuverability and the agility to cast lures and fight fish, respectively. The relative confinement of a Sit-In type yak limits that scope to a degree.

Third Paragraph
(Better argument)

A better argument to support the thesis statement, especially in terms of a safety issue, would be to point out that Sit-On-Top kayaks are self-bailing, whereas Sit-Inside kayaks are not. Once the cockpit of a Sit-Inside yak fills with water, you may find yourself in *deep* trouble. Placing your paragraphs in an ascending order of concern achieves the objective of holding the reader's attention.

Fourth Paragraph
(Best argument)

In terms of arguments of support, always save your best argument for last, for what is said lastly is foremost in the reader's mind. In the classroom, I'll start out by asking students which of the three arguments of support should be presented first in the five-step model: good, better, or best. Invariably, I'll have at least one student say that the 'best' argument should be offered first.
"Why?" I'll ask.
"Because you'll grab the reader's attention," the student will inevitably answer.
"True enough," I'll reply. But then I'll ask, "What happens afterward to the 'good' and 'better' argument?"
Those who didn't see the big picture begin to see the light. The piece would begin to weaken after putting your *best* foot forward; the piece would start to fall apart. You've already presented your 'best' argument, and now the rest becomes watered down.
Let's take a look at an example of a best argument to support the thesis statement before concluding: Sit-On-Top kayaks are safer than Sit-In yaks because if you capsize in a Sit-On-Top kayak, you can upright the vessel and climb back aboard,

whereas with a Sit-Inside type kayak filled with water, you must know and learn self-rescue techniques such as the Eskimo Roll and Paddle Float Rescue. These techniques demand skill, stamina, and strength.

Fifth Paragraph
(Conclusion)

Again, as in the first paragraph, we restate the thesis—but in different words. An example would be to conclude with something along these lines: If you enjoy plying fresh water and/or the suds [salt water] and want the perfect platform, offering both unrestricted casting and catching performance along with peace of mind in terms of safety, a Sit-On-Top kayak is the ultimate angling platform for you. Sit-Inside Kayaks (SINKS) do have their place . . . yes, on the bottom of the list; pun intended.

I'm sure there will be an editor or two who will discourage you from badmouthing Sit-In type kayaks. But in terms of serious fishing and safety, they belong on the bottom of the water column. Therefore, I was being kind in how I phrased myself.

****

Sophisticated Five-Step Model
First Paragraph
(Thesis)

Requisite the aforementioned three- and five-step models, the first paragraph of the sophisticated five-step model, likewise, contains a thesis statement. Once more, we'll stay with kayaks as a topic, modifying the theses viewed in the first and second models so that you can examine yet another approach. Later, we are going to do something quite different. We are going to present the writer as somewhat of an authority on the subject of kayaks. This will be accomplished by eliminating one of the three arguments of support (good, better, best) viewed earlier, substituting it with another approach. Since this will be an elaborate model, we'll place the thesis statement at the end of the first paragraph as a transitional sentence bridging the second paragraph. Instead of discussing selection and safety as such, the thesis will cover design and dependability. Example: For fishing applications, a paddle kayak is a more dependable type of craft than a pedal kayak.

Second Paragraph
(Good argument)

Example: Paddle kayaks have been around forever; pedal kayaks are still in their infancy and, therefore, lack refinement. Hobie (a kayak manufacturer) is the innovator of pedal power kayaks, yet they suffer from a less-than-desirable deck plan for fishing, complicated by the fact that they are difficult to rig.

Third Paragraph
(Rip the Opposition)

    This is the paragraph that makes you look like a pro. You are not only making a statement and supporting it with a good argument in the previous paragraph, you are about to "rip the opposition" by presenting an argument that the proponents of pedal kayaks might use in support of the product. Instead of presenting a second argument in support of paddle kayaks, you are now going to present a *weak* argument that an advocate of pedal versus paddle power might use to bolster his or her contention that pedaling is a better choice than paddling when it comes to fishing. You might be wondering, why present the opposition's argument at all? The answer is that by presenting an argument that an advocate might use in defense of pedaling versus paddling, you are showing that you have considered and understand both sides of the issue. A *weak* argument is easy to shoot down, making you somewhat of an authority —on paper—for who is going to take you to task? Of course, in a live debate, you would never get away with this tactic because the opposition would counter with their good, better, and best arguments as to why pedal power is better than paddle power. But we're not having a live debate. We're writing an article to convince folks that for fishing and safety purposes, a paddle kayak is the way to go.

    Hence, let's examine a *weak* argument one might present via "ripping the opposition" in order to make your presentation more powerful. Example: Referencing angling, proponents of pedal power claim a trolling advantage over paddle power in that pedaling keeps constant tension on the fishing line. This is hardly an argument in favor of purchasing a pedal-type kayak when, in fact, the same momentum is accomplished with a forward paddle stroke.

    I am certainly not going to address the advantages of hands-free operation referencing pedal-type kayaks, which is a proponent's best argument. In truth, paddle and pedal kayaks each have their advantages and disadvantages. It's not a perfect world. However, when weighing the pros and cons relating to fishing applications, paddle kayaks win out over pedal yaks. Period.

Fourth Paragraph
(Best argument)

    The fact that pedal-type kayaks are relatively new, there are design problems. The writer has a good deal of ammunition to posit his best argument. Examples: These pedal-type machines are chain and cable-driven and, therefore, subject to mechanical failure. Consequently, they are difficult to set up, launch, beach, and portage because of their hull design.

Fifth Paragraph
(Conclusion)

Link back to the transitional sentence in your first paragraph, restating the thesis in different words. Example: <u>For fishing applications, pedal kayaks present too many difficulties; therefore, paddle power is more dependable</u>.

****

Review:

Three-step model

Paragraph 1. Thesis statement
Paragraph 2. Good argument to support thesis
Paragraph 3. Conclusion ~ restating thesis by employing different words

Five-step model

Paragraph 1. Thesis statement
Paragraph 2. Good argument to support thesis
Paragraph 3. Better argument to support thesis
Paragraph 4. Best argument to support thesis
Paragraph 5. Conclusion ~ restating thesis by employing different words

Sophisticated Five-Step Model

Paragraph 1. Thesis statement
Paragraph 2. Good argument to support thesis
Paragraph 3. Rip the opposition
Paragraph 4. Best argument to support thesis
Paragraph 5. Conclusion ~ restating thesis by employing different words

****

It is important to develop your paragraphs. Do not shortchange the reader. Elaborate on your thesis, arguments of support, and conclusion. The following article titled **So Many Kayaks—So Little Time ~ How to Choose the Correct Yak** is one of several pieces on the subject that I wrote for *The Fisherman* - Long Island, Metro NY Edition, as well as other well-known fishing publications. Each article had a different theme. I have written much lengthier pieces than the one presented; it all depends on what the publication's guidelines are. Some editors ask for a few hundred words; others may ask for two thousand or more. Several of my articles have been so extensive that they were published in two or three parts, spanning a period of months. The elements covered in this short piece will give you a good idea of additional areas to research and write about on the topic of kayaks, such as necessary equipment, comparable crafts, electronics, et cetera. Keep in mind that the three models presented are simply that—models to guide you through what might otherwise seem a bewildering maze. They are not written in stone. In due time, you are going to come into your own. You will develop your own style of writing and your own way of presenting information.

So Many Kayaks—So Little Time ~ How to Choose the Correct Yak
by Bob Banfelder

It seems that there are more manufacturers and models of kayaks on the market today than Carter has little liver pills. Choosing a yak can be an overwhelming experience. Fortunately, we can immediately narrow the field by focusing in on the single activity that concerns us as readers of *The Fisherman*; and that is, of course, fishing. Look for a kayak from a reputable manufacturer whose selection features or offers optional equipment and accoutrements set up with the angler in mind: flush-mounted rod holders astern, additional fully adjustable-lockable-removable rod holder brackets set forward, a comfortable seat and backrest, ample storage space, an anchor trolley system, rudder system, and a combo unit GPS/Fishfinder. Why all this? Answer: because we ideally want the ultimate fishing platform. By selecting a kayak set up with the angler in mind, we have just ruled out the explorer class, the tandem touring type, and the wild whitewater adventure craft. How come? Answer: because the explorer class calls for a longer, narrower vessel to propel one along greater distances. The tandem touring type is designed for two people to get in each other's way; it is not conducive to fishing. Lastly, the considerably shorter whitewater craft is configured so as to subsume turn-on-a dime maneuverability for psyched-up folks who live to ply swift currents and shoot rapids. Let's now home in on the breed of yak that lends itself to the art of angling—be it spin, bait, or fly-fishing—while at the same time exploring the area of safety. There are basically two types of people-power systems for propelling a kayak: Sit-Ins and Sit-On-Tops. Also, there is a hybrid on the market; that is, a combination of a deep sit-on-top kayak/canoe. Let's briefly examine the trio.

SIT-IN-KAYAKS (SINKs) . . . admittedly taking a bit of liberty with the acronym.

Seemingly, a sit-inside kayak is certainly going to keep you drier than a sit-on-top type. But as safety is predominant, which is the 'safer' vessel between the two? If you are kayaking in an area with heavy boat traffic, I can almost assure you that some so-called captain, either careless or inconsiderate, is going to leave you in his or her wake—a situation that may or may not result in your taking on water or, worse yet, swamping and capsizing you. The cockpit is going to fill, and unless you know a few elaborate safety procedures, you could find yourself in dire straits.

SIT-ON-TOP KAYAKS (SOTs)

Common sense tells you that your season is going to be somewhat limited if you select a sit-on-top kayak, merely because you are going to get wet. You may not want to be braving the elements at the end of November or the middle of March, although you certainly could with the right outfit—namely, a wet suit or dry suit. As the sit-on-top kayak is self-bailing, it is the safer of the two vessels, for it is a relatively simple procedure to climb back aboard if you are capsized. Not so with a sit-in type yak.

SIT-ON-TOP KAYAK/CANOE (the new hybrid)

There's a relatively new kayak on the market that is a combination sit-on-top kayak/canoe (but without scuppers) which is, in essence, a sit-in of sorts. Its freeboard appears impressive and looks as though—as the manufacturer boasts—"very open, yet completely dry." In theory, I like this concept a lot. I'm sure other companies will soon follow suit, but in the meantime, let's take a peek at this innovative kayak-like hull [from Mad River Canoe], conjoined to a canoe-like cockpit.

There are two models. One is the Synergy 12, and is 12 feet long; 30.8 inches wide, and weighs 60 pounds. The other model is the Synergy 14, and is 14 feet long, 30 inches wide, and also weighs 60 pounds. Ostensibly, it appears to offer the best of both worlds.

SPEED vs. STABILITY vs. WEIGHT

I have a savvy fishing acquaintance who raves about his recently purchased Ocean Kayak Prowler 15-foot Angler model. I have a pal who swears by his 13-foot Hobie Quest. I have a fair-weather friend (meteorologically speaking) who simply loves her Wilderness Systems Pamlico 145T (tandem) almost as much as she loves her cat. And that's saying something. The knowledgeable acquaintance I mentioned selected his yak by simply weighing (ah, yes, that too) speed against stability. The 15-foot 4.5-inch long, 28.5-inch wide, 56-pound shell is propelled from point A to point B lickety-split. And that's exactly what the man wants his craft to do; that is, move quickly. I prefer a shorter length and broader beam. My (new for 2007-'08) Ocean Kayak Prowler Big Game Angler measures in at 12 feet 9 inches long, 34 inches wide, and a whopping 69 pounds. That's a 13-pound difference as compared to my acquaintance's craft. That's a lot. But I knew where I was going to use the craft predominately if not exclusively; that is, on the river where we reside as well as its nearby bays—close to our home. Weight, therefore, was not such an important factor. But if I had to transport that vessel from place to place on a regular basis atop my vehicle and/or portage that behemoth a significant distance like some sort of leviathan, it would be the end of the story. And maybe me! So, that beautiful Prowler Big Game kayak is not for everyone. But it is for *moi*. It is a serious fishing machine. Of all the kayaks I researched and sea trialed, few came up to my expectations. Of all the kayaks I could expatiate upon, several kept resurfacing in my notes, my mind, and my very makeup. Two other manufacturers of serious angling platforms to consider are Wilderness System's Tarpon and Malibu Kayak's X-Factor.

RUDDER SYSTEM

Given a fishing application, a rudder is something you may want to seriously consider. Originally, I really didn't entertain a rudder system for my kayak. It was just another mechanical thing to go wrong, I thought. An unnecessary expense, I balked. But the more research I did on the subject, followed by finally operating such a hands-free, foot-operating steering mechanism, the sooner I came to the conclusion that it would come in very handy. Do you really *need* such an amenity? No, you do not. Would it be nice to have such a feature? Surely. Would it aid in fighting a good-size fish? Absolutely. Any counterforce you can apply in battling a brute of a blue or bass, the easier it is going to be to subdue and land your prize. Simply engage your foot pedals to steer accordingly. Maneuvering through tight places, too, where your paddle might otherwise be impeded, is an advantage.

GPS/FISHFINDER

Another important feature I'd consider is a single unit GPS/Fishfinder/transducer. Several kayak companies offer these state-of-the-art combination electronics as part of a package, factory installed. Unless you're fairly handy in working with polyethylene, I'd opt for factory installation. I've seen folks make messes of that system. The unit proves very useful for the serious angler to have such information as the water's depth, surface temperature, thermoclines, bottom structure, speed, lat/lon, compass bearing, waypoints, routes, tracking, and fish symbols at his or her fingertips —to name but a few of the functions these systems can perform. Ah, but do you *need* it? Humm. If you want the added edge, you do.

SELECTING YOUR YAK

Before you run out and purchase the seemingly perfect platform and be accused of impulse buying, you want to know several things. Where are you going to be using your kayak? How do you fit into that form? Are you truly comfortable? How does the vessel track through the water? What type of double-bladed paddle would work to its best advantage? Keep in mind that *not* so age-old adage: different strokes for different folks. In short, no pun intended, consider a short paddle with pronounced curved blades in order for you to execute powerful strokes through some serious swells—such as targeting ocean reefs. Not for the faint of heart. Conversely, select a more conventional, longer handled, narrower-bladed paddle with a flat surface for inshore action. These are all very important considerations. Therefore, 'try before you buy' are words of wisdom. Choice of color, too, is most significant. Do you wish to blend within a serene setting; or do you wish to stand out and be seen for safety's sake? Also, considering what you absolutely *need* to outfit a kayak versus what you would *like* could be worlds apart. Remember, you only have so much space aboard. And for the most part, you take up a good portion of it.

After establishing which configuration is right for you, that is, the sit-inside, sit-on-top, or the hybrid deep sit-on-top/canoe combination, it is equally important to keep three basics in mind when narrowing your selection. Longer, narrower yaks are faster and cover greater distances with less effort. Shorter yaks are lighter and more maneuverable in tight quarters. Wider yaks are more stable platforms. Understanding these three variables and applying them according to the kind of fishing you are going to do will help determine which yak is right for you. Enough yakking. Get out there and rip some lips.

****

If you were writing an article that ran beyond the five-step paragraph model while adhering to the *thesis, good, better, best, conclusion* format, you would simply add additional paragraphs that support your proposition. The method is to build in an ascending order: thesis statement; support with a good argument; follow up with your better argument, continuing with an even better argument than the one preceding it, so on and so forth, saving your best argument for last before concluding.

If you decided to "rip the opposition," you could present that argument somewhere between your first piece of support and your best argument, again, saving your best argument for last before writing the conclusion.

In the following editorial, I present my thesis statement in the first sentence of the first paragraph: **[Richard Tchilinguirian, a twenty-five year old Armenian man, is sitting in prison since August 8, 1990 for a crime he did not commit.]** I continue to build upon that theme. Since I am "ripping the opposition" throughout the piece, in this case the police, I decided to make it part and parcel of my conclusion. Again, the models presented are not scribed in stone; therefore, you may build around them. What I would adhere to, especially for a new writer, is a linear approach to a piece: thesis, support paragraphs in ascending order, and a conclusion linking back to your thesis statement.

The editorial introduced next will give you a clear idea of the arguments presented from *good* to *best*. If I had several arguments to support my thesis but one of them was only fair to middling, I would have to be a big enough person to realize that it was not truly a *good* argument and, therefore, should be discarded. A good argument will hold a reader's attention; a so-so argument might not. Why run the risk?

EDITORIAL: *TOWERS NEWS*, MARCH 1991

POLICE PREVARICATION: THE LONG AND THE SHORT OF IT
by Robert Joseph Banfelder

Richard Tchilinguirian, a twenty-five-year-old Armenian man, is sitting in prison since August 8, 1990 for a crime he did not commit. Richard was convicted of attempted rape; the victim was a twenty-one-year-old Howard Beach girl, Denise Salvaggio, the daughter of an ex-police officer. The crime occurred in October of 1987. The story was first brought to my attention in January of this year via a videotape of Mike Taibbi, CBS-TV News, conducting three consecutive nights of broadcast coverage. This article will drive home several points, positing that Richard Tchilinguirian could not have committed the crime for which he was convicted. It will also illustrate that there are serious flaws in our criminal justice system and that there has been a miscarriage of justice perpetrated by a detective of the 106th Precinct in Queens.

The victim, Denise Salvaggio, had previously identified her attacker from a mug shot at the 112th Precinct, for Richard did have a brush with the law for his minor role as a messenger in a counterfeiting scheme back in 1987. Denise had initially given police a description of her assailant as being 5 feet 8 to 5 feet 9 inches tall, of "slight" build, and weighing approximately 170-175 pounds. However, Richard Tchilinguirian weighs 240 pounds and stands 6 feet 3½ inches tall! 'Stands' is the operative word, as it is quite interesting to note that the detective who made the arrest, Detective Mandel, placed Richard in a sit-down lineup!

In court, when Denise was challenged by Richard's defense attorney as to the initial description given of her attacker as being approximately 5 feet 8 inches, Denise changed her story by adding (and adding is what she did—almost 8 inches), "...five feet eight inches *or taller*," said the 5 foot 9-inch, 110-pound witness for the State. It is also interesting to note that Denise lived with a man who is 6 feet 4 inches tall. Her father. So, Denise would obviously have to stare *up* at her father in order to look him in the eyes as she would have Richard Tchilinguirian. However, Denise stood eye level, staring at her attacker on the night the man approached her on foot. For Denise and the police to say, <u>afterward</u>, that "confusion" was the reason why she dramatically changed her initial description is nothing short of suspect, especially in light of other inconsistencies in her story:

For instance, Denise's friend, Deborah Desario, who accompanied Denise that evening to a discotheque in Manhattan, testified that it was the Palladium on 14th Street that they had visited. But Denise <u>later</u> insisted that it was the 4-D's discotheque on West 54th Street that they had gone to that evening. If that were the case, it would have Denise and Richard 'crossing paths,' for Richard Tchilinguirian was indeed at the 4-D's discotheque, standing on line outside the club before breaking up a fight at 3:00 a.m., the exact time Denise Salvaggio was being attacked by a man she reported as 5 foot 8- to 9-inches tall, 170-175 pounds—approximately 20 miles away. Richard was celebrating a friend's birthday with seven others; that is, eight alibi witnesses who testified that Richard was at the 4-D's discotheque at that particular hour. Three key witnesses took polygraphs, the results of which concluded that they were "not attempting deception"; the two young women, Denise and Deborah, did not take such a test. Furthermore, there were two other witnesses, a father and son of Scottie's Car Care, located next door to the now defunct 4-D's discotheque in Manhattan, who were not questioned until after the trial but also swore that Richard Tchilinguirian was on line breaking up a fight. Not surprisingly, the bouncer at the discotheque also remembered Richard.

The plot thickens when we learn that Deborah Desario said she saw a man about 5 foot 8- or 9- inches tall, "slight" build, 170 pounds, standing by a phone booth near her home in Ozone Park where Denise dropped her off before heading home to Howard Beach, moments before the attack took place. In other words, Richard Tchilinguirian had to have been omnipresent, standing on line at the 4-D's discotheque in Manhattan, standing at a phone booth in Ozone Park, then beating Denise back to her home in Howard Beach in time to approach and attempt to violate her. And, like an evil anti-super hero of sorts, Richard Tchilinguirian had to have changed clothing (in that very phone booth, perhaps) from head to toe, for all respective parties note that Richard Tchilinguirian was garbed in a dark shirt, dress slacks and shoes whereas the perpetrator wore a Yankee jacket, jeans and sneakers as attested to by Denise, her friend Deborah, and, as you will learn in just a moment, an actual eyewitness to the attack.

The direction from where this miscarriage of justice dramatically but demonically casts its light is upward, illuminating the likes of Detective Mandel and those public servants who pervert and pollute our so-called criminal justice system—pervert it with their lies and pollute it by their omissions of truths. For Detective Richard Mandel withheld pertinent information involving the Tchilinguirian case, then later lied about it. The detective had questioned an actual eyewitness to the attack, the next-door neighbor of the Salvaggio's, Nicholas Loukas, and learned that the description Nick gave matched the description initially given by Denise and Deborah. During the bail hearing, Detective Mandel claimed that he had an eyewitness who implicated Richard Tchilinguirian in another case that the detective was investigating. This was later proven to be untrue. Detective Mandel has a history of such tactics and had purportedly been involved in the murder of his mistress after she threatened to leave him. This certainly raises serious questions as to the competence of our law enforcement officials. Detective Mandel has subsequently been discredited and forced to retire, but with full pension, I might add. Remarkably, he had been assigned to the Queens District Attorney's office.

What many citizens fail to realize is how easy it is to indict. The cliché bantered about the hallowed halls of court is that "you can indict a ham sandwich." A good many folks fail to realize that it is the job of the cop to build a case for the DA, and build a case he or she does. It is the job of the DA, and nothing less than that, to win the case—at any expense. This writer can attest to the lies, deception, and manipulation presented by the police, detectives of the 112th Precinct's Queens Sex Crimes Unit (of which I have previously reported as being "out of control"), as well as bureau chiefs and assistant district attorneys involving other cases in Queens County since 1983. As a matter of fact, one could almost see their very noses grow, inches at a clip. I think it's high time that we, the people, stop these official offenders. I think it's high time that Geppetto put Pinocchio through the would-be mill. What say ye, Governor? Get this innocent young man out of jail today!

Robert Joseph Banfelder teaches English at Queensborough Community College—writes about our criminal justice system—and is the author of a psychological thriller titled *Dicky, Richard, and I*.

****

[**Note:** I wrote eight editorials/articles concerning the Tchilinguirian matter for *Towers News*. I believe you will find it interesting to learn that the sentencing judge, Judge Ralph Sherman, overturned Richard's guilty verdict. Richard Tchilinguirian was released from prison on February 4th, 1992, having served 16 months in prison for a crime he did not commit.]

Let's look back to the importance of proper punctuation. The following is a grammar textbook review that I had written for the English Department at Queensborough Community College, Bayside, New York. It was published in the *Queensborough Review ~ A Journal About Writing* (circa 1983). The three examples excerpted from Carl Markgraf's grammar text are an excellent illustrations of confusion converted to clearness.

A Grammar Textbook Review
by Professor Robert Banfelder

Simply *telling* students that punctuation is important in clearly communicating their intended meaning is about as illuminating as casually mentioning that Diogenes went around Athens in search of an honest man. Only when students *see* that the philosopher's search was aided by a lantern—in broad daylight—do they catch a glimpse of the Athenian's cynicism. Further exemplification illuminates Diogenes as a cynic, for when Alexander the Great offered the non-materialistic Diogenes anything he wanted, the philosopher's only request was that Alexander step aside to prevent his blocking the sunlight. This overview depicts Diogenes as a virtuous man who simply could not find another whose measure of excellence met his own exceedingly high standards.

Showing students how faulty punctuation—not to mention the lack of any punctuation—confuses intended meaning is well exemplified in Carl Markgraf's

Punctuation—A Self-Teaching Guide. The author's examples are so overwhelmingly clear and abundant that students are actually amazed at the multiformity of meaning. The following is but a sampling.

1. simply confusing:

My cousin Jim asked me to set Mr. Fitch's barn afire and I said I would not understanding that it might get me into trouble the night of the fire I went home and talked about Mr. Fitch to my brother and my cousin Jim had a drink and went out and set fire to the barn.

2. guilty narrator:

My cousin Jim asked me to set Mr. Fitch's barn afire, and I said I would, not understanding that it might get me into trouble. The night of the fire I went home and talked about Mr. Fitch to my brother and my cousin Jim, had a drink and went out and set fire to the barn.

3. guilty cousin:

My cousin Jim asked me to set Mr. Fitch's barn afire, and I said I would not, understanding that it might get me into trouble. The night of the fire I went home and talked about Mr. Fitch to my brother, and my cousin Jim had a drink and went out and set fire to the barn.

Of course, the above may seem an oversimplified view of comma sense; but common sense, with a gradual step-by-step hands-on approach presented in a non-threatening and rule-restrictive role is the format of Markgraf's practical guide.

In short, Markgraf sheds a luminous intensity upon the elements of punctuation, helping the beginning writer to overcome both fear and frustration. The virtue of this book lies in its simplicity, for Professor Markgraf has pushed aside the dark cloud of confusion to let the sun shine through.

Professor Robert J. Banfelder
(English Department)

Carl Markgraf, Punctuation—A Self-teaching Guide (New York: John Wiley & Sons, 1979), p.36.

****

You now have several important models to help guide you through your writing projects. Having absorbed these lessons up to this point, you are very close to starting your own writing project to send off for consideration, be it a Letter to the Editor of your local newspaper, a report for a newsletter, perhaps an article for a magazine, et cetera. You're probably anxious to do just that. However, I would like for you to hold off querying or sending anything out until you finish *all* these lessons. I want you to present your work in the best possible light. That doesn't mean you can't get started drafting a piece—if you haven't already.

LESSON 11

Taking a Spell

Let's now take a detour (sorry, there are no shortcuts) away from that minefield-laden landscape abominably referred to as *grammar* and head into an area equally filled with pitfalls and an occasional pothole; namely, *spelling*.

Confession time: I am a terrible speller. I state this fact to my students early on in the hope that they will not give up on themselves . . . especially the guys. Guys are generally, for some ungodly reason, ghastly spellers. Girls, by and large, have the spelling bee part of their brain well-developed. Concerning both genders, this conjecture of mine carries over into adulthood: females are usually good spellers; males are not. Unfortunately, fellows, there is no panacea. However, there are helpful techniques to be applied. This does not mean that females are allowed to *skirt* these lessons. They are being presented to help everyone—male or female.

As mentioned previously, there are <u>a lot</u> (not alot) of pitfalls in writing that will make you look bad if you are not careful. Perhaps carelessness has nothing to do with it; quite possibly you are genuinely not aware of certain spelling problems that plague a good many writers. Case in point: I know editors of publications who will not read <u>past</u> (not passed) the first paragraph of a submitted piece if they see the kind of errors shown <u>here</u> (not hear.) Why? To be quite blunt, those mistakes are quite common among *new* writers, pigeonholing you as an <u>amateur</u> (not amature). Frankly, an editor does not have the time to spend correcting the many mistakes that are sure to follow in light of what he or she has seen in the first paragraph or on the first page. You might not think this is fair, especially if the content of your article is nothing less <u>than</u> (not then) great. If you fail to handle the proper usage of *their, there,* and *they're,* well, <u>it's</u> (not its) probably over for you at the starting gate. To think for a moment that the art of well-written prose has lost <u>its</u> (not it's) appeal—think again. Granted, some educators wish to relax certain rules; true educators see the fallacy in this because it creates a domino <u>effect</u> (effect [noun] not affect [verb]). We may argue the point until the cows come home, but the fact of the matter is that you have a far better chance of getting your work published if you adhere to the basic <u>principles</u> (not principals) underlying accepted usage, both in terms of grammar and spelling.

These above examples will give you some idea of why, at the end of Lesson 10, I had asked you to hold off on submitting a piece for publication until you complete this twelve-lesson course. I want you to hone (not home) your writing skills before doing so—so that you will scintillate and give yourself the added edge.

Memorization

I make a joke concerning the fact that I have a good memory but that it is rather short. Pure and simple memorization never really worked for me, but applying tricks, gimmicks and such to *help* me memorize troublesome words does work. Case in point: I could never remember how to spell the word *across*. Does it have one or two *c's* and *s's*? But by picturing a person carrying *a cross* across a street, planted the image and the correct spelling firmly in my mind. Granted, your computer's Spell Check program will pick up such a mispelling simply because it *is* misspelled as shown in red. But do not forget that spelling demons such as *their*, *there*, and *they're* will not be flagged if used incorrectly. For example: [Their are many spelling demons that are not noted on Spell Check; their they're to trip you up and take you down a notch.] Again, note that *their*, *there* and *they're* in the bracketed example are misspelled and that the computer would not necessarily pick up these errors.

The techniques you employ in order to keep these demons from taking you down into an abyss are not written in stone. Use whatever method works for you. It may be an image that you bring to mind such as the example of a cross being carried across a street. Other times you may have to rely on sheer memory.

The word *their*, has an i in it. It shows possession and should help you to remember its meaning: 'belonging to them.' Example: It was their turn.

The word *there* can mean the following ~ in, at, or to that place; in that respect.

Correct examples: The book is over there. There is a time to work, and there is a time to play.

They're is the contraction for 'they are.' In other words, the two words are drawn together to form a shortened version. Example: They're going to the store.

Though you may or may not be familiar with the examples cited, I use them to illustrate some important points. To rely solely on one's memory is a *big* mistake, for how many megabytes, gigabytes, or terabytes can the human brain compute, especially if you are suffering a migraine, regardless of which hemisphere of your gourd is under attack. In elementary school, we were told to carry a list of *all* the words that we found troublesome and to commit them to memory. I carried around a thick pocket dictionary and explained to the teacher that I had crossed out approximately a hundred or so words I was confident of spelling correctly while having the remainder serve as my *list*. Neither Ms. Charm nor I thought that was very funny. The class, however, positively roared.

I'm about to let you in on a little-known secret. It's how I go about writing when I'm working on the computer. I will not interrupt my work by leaving the desktop page for even a moment to go onto an online dictionary. Nor will I take the trouble to start looking up the spelling of a word in my unabridged dictionary that sits immediately to my right. Why? Quite candidly, I could experience the frustration of failing to find the word that I was searching for—phonetically. Examples: homonym or homophone. I would be wasting my time hunting for the incorrect spellings of ha·ma·nim or hom·e·phone. But by simply typing in virtually *any* phonetic spelling of words on my Franklin Dictionary & Thesaurus Language Master unit, which sits adjacent to my computer keyboard, I can instantly note the correct spelling and meaning of the word I am searching. I do this without having to shift screens between my prose and the computer's (online) dictionary. This is very important to me. In most cases, I can hit the Franklin's synonym and thesaurus mode keys and retrieve a list of similar words and expressions. This is a great tool when trying to summon the right word that is on the tip of your tongue but has escaped you for the moment or altogether. This linguistic technology, offered by Franklin/Merriam-Webster, measuring 5 x 7 x ½-1½ inches, is an electronic (4 AA batteries) gem. My young son bought me the unit many years ago and, no differently than my Timex watch, that minicomputer keeps right on ticking. A similar unit today costs in the neighborhood of $60.

In elementary school and high school, several teachers had us keep long lists of vexatious words. I'd remember the spelling just long enough to pass any weekly test with flying colors. The following week, we'd be given a new list of words. On and on these examinations continued until it was time to be tested on *all* the words we had learned over the course of months. Hundreds of words were given to us at a single clip. This time out, I didn't do so well. Again, good memory, which grew short, I'd joke. We then had to put our misspelled words on flashcards—correct spelling on one side, brief definition of the word on the reverse side of the card. My tall stack resembled card games requiring two standard decks of playing cards. This went on throughout the school year. What I experienced in addition to utter frustration was the sensation of heat rising through my neck to my cheeks. It was interesting to note that most of the boys experienced this condition as opposed to the girls. Once more, the girls in the class fared (not faired) far better than the boys.

Then there were those teachers who applied different methods of teaching, or trying to teach, spelling. These well-intentioned men and women breathed and lived by a set of *rules*: spelling rules. They talked and chalked their way across a long blackboard, scribbling down a list of words that contained double letters and how to handle them, or ranted on endlessly about those rather distressing *e i* and *i e* combinations. I had believed for a brief moment that I was finally able to follow, grasp, and hold onto a bit of this arcane business of *rules*. I liked that concept a lot. However, I quickly learned that once I had this mysterious language concerning the arrangement of letters finally figured out, or so I thought, I soon discovered that there were a series of exceptions to these so-called *rules*.

Later in life I realized that many of these lessons were learned by rote, best defined as the habitual, mechanical, and oftentimes monotonous performance of study —no different than having learned my ABCs. Hence, a quick remedial lesson referencing that frequently troublesome *e i* and *i e* relationship, presented along with a list of exceptions to the rule, is in order.

Use *i* before *e* except after *c*, or when sounded like a long *a* as in the words eight, weigh, neighbor. Remember that rule from school? If not, this one rather simple rule will help you considerably.

Here are a few examples that follow the rule:

i **before** *e* ach**ie**ve, bel**ie**ve, br**ie**f, ch**ie**f, f**ie**ld, f**ie**rce, fr**ie**nd, gr**ie**ve.

i **before** *e* ***except immediately after c*** c**ei**ling, conc**ei**t, conc**ei**ve, dec**ei**t, perc**ei**ve, rec**ei**pt, rec**ei**ve.

e **before** *i* **when sounded like a long** *a* **ei**ght, chow m**ei**n, fr**ei**ght, n**ei**ghbor, r**ei**gn, r**ei**ndeer, v**ei**n, w**ei**gh.

If you did not adhere to this rule, you would have to rely on tricks. Example: Do you bel<u>ie</u>ve the lie? This might help you remember the correct spelling of the word believe.

Now, here's the rub. As mentioned, there are exceptions to the rule. The word **weird** is spelled correctly, yet it does not follow the *i* before *e* rule; there is no *c* before *ei*, which would signal us to reverse those two letters. Telling yourself, "That's weird," will help you remember the exception to the rule. Unfortunately, there is a list of words that do not follow the rule. Words like *ancient, conscience, conscientious, deficient, efficient, omniscient, proficient*, and *sufficient*. Note that they contain the letters *cien*. Still, there is an additional list of words, exceptions, too, to the *i, e, c* rule that violates the law. Words such as *caffeine, codeine, counterfeit, either, financier, foreign, forfeit, height, leisure, neither, protein, science, seize*, and back to the word *weird*. It's all very frustrating, to say the least. But among systems and tools such as a computer's Spell Check, an electronic Dictionary/Thesaurus like the Franklin Language Master, and an unabridged dictionary—most necessary tools of the trade—I'm able to stay out of that abyss of spelling demons. You will, too. Admittedly, most of the troublesome words that I spell correctly, without any aid, I learned by rote as opposed to a set of rules. Rather than burden you with too many rules, I've kept the most important rules and their exceptions to a minimum.

In order to fully comprehend the next lesson, it is important that you have a brief but basic spelling vocabulary. As this is a Basic to Beyond (advanced) guidebook, I feel it is essential to now and again inject certain fundamentals that you may have missed somewhere along life's path. It might have been as simple as being absent on the day your grammar teacher covered **prefixes**, **roots**, and **suffixes**. A good friend of mine would half-kiddingly say to me that he was absent on the day the teacher taught and then handed out patience. In an earlier lesson of this guidebook (dealing with alliteration), we covered **vowels** (a, e, i, o, u, and sometimes y—representing a vowel sound); **consonants** (a sound other than a vowel: b, c, d, f, et cetera); **syllables** (letters or groups of letters representing a unit of sound). Every syllable *must* have a vowel sound.

A **root** (not route) is the main part of the word to which a prefix or suffix may be connected.

A **prefix** is a group of letters that comes before a root.

A **suffix** is a letter or group of letters that comes after the root.

    Example: **prefix**   **root**   **suffix**
               dis   appear   ance =   disappearance

The Art of Doubling

Adding prefixes to the entire root word:

When the prefix ends with the same letter that begins the root word, keep the double letters.

Adding suffixes to the entire root word:
When the suffix begins with the same letter that ends the root word, keep the double letters.

    Example: mispell (word spelled incorrectly)
             [root word] spell
            [prefix] mis
            misspell (word spelled correctly)

    Example: overun (word spelled incorrectly)
             [root word] over
            [suffix] run
            overrun (word spelled correctly)

Let's reexamine the word *disappearance* used a moment ago: Note that the word contains a prefix, root word, and a suffix.

    Example: **prefix**   **root**   **suffix**
               dis   appear   ance =   disappearance

Note, too, that there are <u>no</u> double letters connected to the root word because the prefix *dis* does <u>not</u> end with the same letter that begins the root word.
Note, also, that there are <u>no</u> double letters connected to the root word because the suffix does <u>not</u> begin with the same letter that ends the root word.

Once more, let's review the rules referencing prefixes, root words, and suffixes.

Adding prefixes to the entire root word:

When the prefix ends with the same letter that begins the root word, keep the double letters.

Adding suffixes to the entire root word:
When the suffix begins with the same letter that ends the root word, keep the double letters.

Take a break (not brake) before moving into the next lesson. You earned a breathing spell.

Changing *y* to *i*

Here is a simple rule to bear (not bare) in mind with words ending in *y*:
When words end with the letter *y* preceded by a consonant, you change the *y* to *i* before adding suffixes, <u>except</u> when the suffix begins with the letter *i*.
In the following example, the *y* in *cry* is, indeed, preceded by a consonant letter, which is **r**. Therefore, you retain the *y* in *cry* and add the *ing* suffix.

Example: cry
[root word] cry
[suffix] ing
crying (word spelled correctly)

In order to better understand this lesson, it would be a good time to introduce a short list of some of the most common suffixes. First, we'll examine three suffixes (ed, ing, es) so as to see how they apply to our root word *cry*.

ed	ing	es
cried	crying	cries

With the *ed* suffix connected to the word *cry* you will note, according to the rule, that the *y* gets changed to *i* before the suffix is added. Hence, the word *cried* is spelled correctly.
With the *ing* suffix connected to the word cry you will note, according to the rule, that you retain the *y* and add the suffix. Hence, the word *crying* is spelled correctly.
With the *es* suffix connected to the word *cry* you will note, according to the rule, that the *y* gets changed to *i* before the suffix is added. Hence, the word *cries* is spelled correctly.

Here is a listing of commonly used <u>suffixes</u>, including those already covered: able, al, ed, er, es, est, hood, ible, ic, ing, ly, ment, ness, ous, s, ship, tion, y. In the first example, *able* is connected to its root word *comfort* to form the entire word comfortable. In the last example, *y* is connected to its root word *gloom* to form the entire word gloomy.
Here is a listing of commonly used <u>prefixes</u>: ante, anti, co, dis, extra, hyper,

grand, il, im, in, inter, ir, mal, mis, non, pre, semi, ultra, un, uni. In the first example, *ante* is connected to its root word *room* to form the entire word anteroom. In the last example, *uni* is connected to its root word *cycle* to form the entire word unicycle.

Proofreading

As a good writer, one of the most important responsibilities you have is to proofread what you have written before sending it out to be considered for publication. The key to doing this is to start fresh. To finish writing a piece and begin proofing and editing is a waste of time because the mind is probably tired. Proofing your work off the computer is fine for an initial first read. Later, however, you should print out your work as a hard copy to be proofed anew by placing a ruler below each and every line. This method will not only slow you down (which you must do), it will also force you to focus on a limited number of, not only words, but letters. You want your field of vision narrowed to approximately six letters at a clip. Use the retracted point of a pen or pencil to touch each syllable upon the printed page. You are not *reading*, per se: you are *proofing* your piece. You are looking for trouble: spelling, grammar, punctuation problems, et cetera. You *will* find errors.

Leave no stone unturned. Concentrate.

Now, for the *piecè de résistance*. Once you are satisfied that you have caught any and all errors, you truly haven't. Trust me. It is time for you to *read* your work—**aloud!** Your ears will catch what your eyes have failed to find. The trick is to *read* what is *actually* before you—not what *should* be there—written upon the printed page. You will most likely find a syntactical problem; that is, the way in which you string your words together. Example: Leave stone unturned. I had inadvertently omitted the word *no* from the sentence. Guess what? The computer failed to pick up my omission. The sentence should read Leave no stone unturned. Furthermore, staying on a syntactical tact, you would want to examine the sense of the sentence. Is it logical? Example: In the above paragraph, I had <u>*originally*</u> written as a draft: Use the tip of a pen or pencil to touch each syllable upon the printed page. In terms of the sentence's syntactical construction, it's fine. However, in terms of sentence sense, something is wrong. Think carefully. A pencil's tip is not retractable unless it's a mechanical pencil. Also, if the tip weren't retractable, it would make unnecessary marks upon the printed page. Be that careful in your thinking. Proofreading is a demanding but important skill. The cleaner your submission, the better chance you have of becoming published.

In our next lesson, we'll be looking at making decent dollars by writing articles for various publications.

LESSON 12

Talking It Up—During and After Publication

It all began with the Richard Tchilinguirian case cited earlier. I wrote those nine editorials for *Towers News*, pro bono. I donated my time (lots of it) and energy (indefatigable persistence) to a cause I believed in wholeheartedly: the exoneration and release of an innocent young man from prison. I can well-imagine that one of the most frightening experiences a person can endure is being arrested, convicted, and sentenced to prison for a crime he or she did not commit. What is equally alarming is when law enforcement personnel fail to do their job, allowing such events to take place. Such was the situation with Richard Tchilinguirian. The young man was innocent of the crime for which he was arrested, convicted, and sentenced to prison; how utterly horrible. I made it my business to do something about this matter. So did several other fine folks.

After Richard's guilty verdict was overturned, and he was finally released from prison, I insisted on being paid for future writing assignments with *Towers News*. After all, I had proven myself by drawing a good deal of attention to the egregious behavior of the police and other law enforcement personnel. The first form of payment I received from my boss at *Towers News* was a *free* lunch at a restaurant for a review that I had written for the eatery. That did not cut it. I politely explained to my publisher that there was no such thing as a truly *free* lunch, and that I wanted to be paid in dollars or *dinero*. She smiled demurely, finally agreeing to pay me a paltry $50 dollars per editorial and/or article. At least I was getting and keeping my name out there, writing about several sensational cases that had made national headlines.

From the early to the late nineties, I continued to write about our criminal justice system: John Gotti, noted mobster and boss of the Gambino crime family in New York; Amy Fisher, dubbed the "Long Island Lolita" who attempted to kill Mary Jo Buttafuoco, wife of Joey Buttafuoco; Joey Buttafuoco, an auto body-shop owner who made headlines for his affair with the underage girl, Amy Fisher; Leona Helmsley, billionaire hotel magnate, convicted on federal tax evasion charges—having served 18 months in prison. The woman was dubbed the "Queen of Mean"; Kerry Kotler, defendant in a Long Island rape case. New DNA technology excluded the convicted man, yet Suffolk County District Attorney James M. Catterson, Jr. fiercely fought the scientific community's findings; Katie Beers' kidnapping case–culprit, John Esposito; Galen Kelly, cult deprogrammer; Salvatore (Sammy the Bull) Gravano, Mafia underboss of the Gambino crime family, noted for bringing down John Gotti; JonBenét Ramsey, famous unsolved murder.

Also, I took a jab or two (pun intended) at Mike Tyson, a heavyweight who needs no introduction anent his fights both inside and outside the boxing ring. Off the football field, I tackled the darling of denial, Orenthal James Simpson re the Nicole Brown Simpson (O.J.'s wife) and Ron Goldman murder trial. At my publisher's insistence, I even did a snapshot piece on UFOs. The sum total of what I made from writing these editorials/articles, editorials, and follow-up pieces at least kept me in gas money to run my twenty-five foot boat. That was my rationalization. The price of gas for the nineties was nothing compared to what I would need for the new millennium.

Writing numerous pieces on the many facets of both freshwater and saltwater fishing (spin, bait, fly), inclusive of fly-tying recipes, netted me somewhere in the neighborhood of $150 to $175 per article. I followed up with boating articles (power, sail, canoe, kayak); waterfowl shooting; gun and bowhunting for white-tailed deer; target shooting (handguns, shotguns, rifles); the art of smoking fish, fowl, and game; product reviews (fly lines, et al, rods, reels and lures); electric and charcoal water smokers. I wrote a travel piece that we covered earlier, referencing Greenport—a charming seaport village. If a prospective article could be connected to the great outdoors with regard to woods or water, I probably wrote about it.

Now and again there will be some overlap among your themes; this makes writing your next article a bit easier. Just don't submit the same article accepted by one publisher to another publisher. That's a no-no. You're not syndicated in this sense. Not uncommonly, once you have established yourself with an editor and built a good rapport, you may be asked to write an article on a particular subject the publication is after. For instance, I was asked if I would write a piece on the new ethanol-blended gasoline and its effect on marine engines; another, on the cost effectiveness of offshore windmills. Occasionally, I'd score with a check for $400 to $700 as when I interviewed and wrote about Jenny Mundus, wife of the world-famous shark fisherman, Frank Mundus. All told and tallied, that proved to be a good amount of gas money to feed my vessel. Timely stories that I couldn't sell, I submitted freely to various organizations' newsletters; for example, The New York Sportfishing Federation, or angling clubs such as Eastern Flyrodders of Long Island. Other pieces were offered in the form of Letters to the Editor of local newspapers—once again, keeping my name out there before the public. Affiliating yourself with organizations, clubs, and the media will give you a good deal of exposure. As Donna and I do dine out regularly, you can pick up a few extra dollars by writing an occasional restaurant review. You won't get rich, and you may put on extra pounds, but at least you'll offset the cost of a meal or two. Again, I do this more to keep my *name* in the forefront, not my *belly*. After having several restaurant reviews published, I came close to writing a food column for a fishing magazine. The editor was all in favor of it, but the publisher shot down the proposal. You never know, though, so follow through on your ideas. You have nothing to lose—weight-wise or otherwise. Eventually, I got to write a monthly column for an online fishing magazine. Ultimately, I was offered my own Cablevision show, which I co-host with Donna, my life's partner.

When my award-winning novels were hot off the press, I'd query newspapers to see if they wanted to do an interview and photo shoot. My query was often followed by a most positive response. There were times I'd take on and write about a controversial topic, make appearances on local and national television shows, give talks and lectures at local libraries, which averaged $150. Most recently, I gave myself a raise, elevating my fee to $200 a talk. I offer to address a range of subjects, including the writing process (basic to advanced writing skills), getting published, the serial-killer phenomena, our criminal justice system, and consumer advocacy (covering an imposing group of strategies). I started teaching this latter course as part of an Evening Adult Education Program that I designed at Queensborough Community College, where I instructed several writing classes for more than a decade. Stimulating and rewarding were my achievements in an intellectual sense, not necessarily in any monetary respect. But that was fine for the moment. As my chairperson would say to me from time to time, "Robert, do you truly expect to lead a charmed life?" Well, I do try.

My novels sold when I appeared at a bookstore for a book signing, otherwise they sat on those shelves collecting dust. Although printed by legitimate publishers and hailed as award-winners by genuine reviewers, the books were published by small presses and reviewed by bantam companies. It's a tough business. The success I have had and still enjoy is not measured by a monetary barometer. However, I had more than sufficient funds to run my boat and fuel my passion for fishing with needed accessories. As gas prices steadily rose, I simply wrote more articles.

In March of 2010, I launched a series of publications (one of which you are presently reading in book form). This kept me quite busy. Coupled to my nine novels and three nonfiction books, which may be purchased online at Amazon, I feel I've made a dent and a difference. You can, too. The key to this whole business is to enjoy what you're doing. Find *your* niche and follow your dream. Without having deprived my family or myself, I initially pursued my main interest (writing) part time before making it a full-time endeavor. I won't find myself in later life saying, "Coulda, woulda, shoulda." I'm giving it my best shot and, once again, *you* can, too. Your attempt may only start out as a hobby and/or as a way to supplement your income (modestly). Then one day, like a child straddling a hobbyhorse, you could find yourself racing toward the finish line—a winner in your own right!

Keep in mind that sharp photographs of the subject matter you are writing about will help sell your article to an editor/publisher. Conversely, a photographer who can write well will increase his or her chances of having a piece accepted by presenting a cogent paragraph or two to accompany the photo(s). If you were writing a gardening piece, support photos would certainly help capture the essence of your topic. I usually submit several photographs with my article. If you do not have a sharp photo to accompany the piece, chances are that the editor and/or publisher may have one in their archive. My point is to not let the lack of a picture discourage you from submitting work. Bear in mind that an editor/publisher will sometimes pay extra per image. When submitting a fly-fishing story that included a step-by-step fly-tying recipe, I received almost the same amount of money for the photos as I did the piece. Learning how to take good photographs is not at all difficult. Learning how to take great photos comes with knowledge and know-how, patience and practice, and perhaps a bit of luck—meaning, being in the right place at the right time. Whenever folks viewed my photo albums, they commented, "You're a pretty good photographer, Bob," to which I would reply: "Seems so. Actually, I take a score of shots of the same subject, choose the best one, place it in the album, cancel or discard the rest." That was my so-called secret for getting a good photograph. However, with a film camera, I was limited as to how many shots I could take before it became cost prohibitive, but with a digital camera, the sky's the limit.

Without even intentionally networking, you will be surprised how one thing leads to another. Case in point: A couple of years after I interviewed and wrote up a few Mundus pieces, Frank Mundus passed away. The captain's famed vessel, the *Cricket II*, now had a new owner. I contacted the Rhode Island/Connecticut-based captain through Jenny Mundus, who had put the boat out to bid. As a result of contacting the gentleman who won the bid, I got an interview and sold the story. Down the pike, I sold a second piece referencing its new captain, Jon Dodd, and the renowned *Cricket II*.

Following a publisher's guidelines is of paramount importance. If an editor asks for between 1,200 and 2,000 words, do not submit 1,000 words. Conversely, if he or she asks for a maximum of 2,000 words, do not send 3,000 words. If your article turns out rather lengthy, you could ask if the piece might be considered for publication in two parts. I have had many two- and three-part articles accepted. If you are asked to write an article on a topic with which you are unfamiliar, try not to pass up this opportunity. Sure, we would all rather write about what we know; still, if you are not acquainted with a certain subject matter, reluctant to take on the assignment, get over your apprehension—go for it! Research the topic to death then write the article. This, understandably, takes a great deal of work. On completion of the piece, you will probably come away with the feeling that it wasn't worth your time and effort—monetarily. This kind of thinking is a mistake. When I was asked to write those articles on ethanol gasoline and offshore windmills mentioned earlier, I knew next to nothing about the two subjects. Nevertheless, I accepted the challenge. When I finished researching, writing and having the piece accepted, I had accomplished three things. One, it broadened my horizon. Two, it put me in contact with experts in the field who invited me to call on them at any time—networking at its finest. Three, I was building a solid relationship with my editor. Try and put aside the negative notion concerning the number of hours spent researching and writing such an article divided into a paltry payment. Granted, I was only making a few dollars an hour. On a more positive note, shortly thereafter, the same editor called on me to write two articles on a topic I know something about: surf fishing and offshore fishing. I put together an article with regard to relatively new *systems* and *techniques* with which many people here in the United States are unfamiliar. I could hardly wait to get my greedy little hands on the *promotional* rod, reel, line, and lures a company sent me. More on this subject in the next and final lesson; it's going to be an eye-opener for a good number of folks.

Standing back from the information I just unfolded, you cannot tell me that you'd be hard-pressed to find a topic on which to write. Start by brainstorming what you enjoy most in your spare time. Perhaps you like tinkering with automobile engines, or back to the scene of working in your garden. Have you found a better way of growing something? What are you good at that you can share with a readership? There is most definitely a magazine or journal that covers your area of interest. You probably even subscribe to the periodical. Go through the pages carefully, perusing not only what interests you, but see what other types of articles the publication includes. This approach may spark an idea. Also, don't be afraid to think outside the box. Case in point: Why would a saltwater fishing magazine find interest in an article on Swimming Pool Noodles? Let's see why. The following is an article that I wrote and was published in *Nor'east Saltwater*, a magazine for which I freelance articles on the first and second of every month and have for many years. Accompanying the article were several photographs, which helped sell the story.

Using Your Noodle
by Bob Banfelder

The idea for this *Using Your Noodle* article came about through several sound knocks upon my noggin as I would enter and leave the cabin of our twenty-two foot pilothouse. Actually, the impression was both literally and figuratively formed when I practically cracked open my skull one evening while scurrying through the hatch in search of a pair of longnose pliers in order to remove a well-embedded hook from the gullet of a schoolie striper.

"I've got to figure a way to pad the top of that bloody @%##&* door!" I told Donna in a single sentence, incorporating a string of expletives that would have filled this page from top to bottom.

"Bloody, indeed!" she exclaimed, seemingly more concerned about the bloody mess atop the hatch and the sanguinous pool upon the deck. "Poor fish," she lamented.

"Does that @%##&* blood belong mainly to me or the fish?" I questioned through clenched teeth, trying to quell the pain through profanity and self-pity.

"Both. Give me those," she demanded, taking the pliers and deftly removing the hook from the throat of the nearly legal beauty, placing the fish back into the water. "Now, let's have a look at that head, Ishmael," she said, sighing with annoyance.

"Very funny."

"Not as funny as what you wanted to do to that poor fish with those pliers."

It was a day or two later when we were in White's Bait-Tackle & Fly Shop, off of Front Street in Greenport. Ken Birmingham, Jr. ran the shop as well as operated Surf & Turf Charters, located in back of the building. It was there that I spied the 28-foot Parker with a piece of foam fixed across the top of the hatchway.

"Where did you get that foam section, and how did you attach it to the frame?" I begged the question, rubbing my still sore skull as a firm reminder.

"That? That's a Noodle, like you see in swimming pools. My tall customers and I got tired of banging our heads," he explained.

"Tell me about it." I showed him my cut through the hair.

"Ouch; that's a nice slice you got there, Bob. Come. I'll show you what I did, which took me thirty seconds and cost me about a buck."

Ken took us inside the shop, grabbed a Noodle, and illustrated the simple solution to my problem while Donna browsed about in search of tackle that might take down Moby Dick.

Instructions:

Simply measure and cut the length of foam tubing that you need for the top of the hatch. Then, setting the blade of the utility knife to the correct depth, slice the Noodle lengthwise to its hollow core. Slip the section atop the doorframe and/or any hanging overhead strip as pictured in the photo. You are done. However, if you are anal, as I admittedly am, and enjoy turning a simple procedure into a project, you can measure and cut the length needed by wrapping a piece of masking tape around both ends of the tube for perfectly even cuts. Just remember to cut on the correct side of the tape, using its edge as your guide. Too, you can run a marking pen along the length of the tube with a straightedge for the flawless slice.

Additionally, if you wish to have those most often used streamer flies or other lures at the ready, simply cut a section and find a place for it aboard your vessel— either in the cockpit or cabin or both. I managed to find a spot at one end of my chart table, tucked beneath a shelf as indicated in the next photo. Actually, to have the tube positioned securely, I placed another behind it as a filler. By using your *noodle*, the one between your ears, you can be creative and surely find a location to utilize empty or useless space. The store-bought noodle serves very nicely in having those artificials close at hand and not embedded in one, as the foam strip protects both you and your arsenal.

Finally, I found the perfect solution to my over-the-gunwale boarding ladder storage problem. There's a shelf up forward of the V-berth, which is about the only place I can stow the ladder without it being underfoot. As I really don't use it often, that shelf is the ideal place. However, it is so positioned that the ladder falls down whenever we hit rough water. I've tried wedging it, even bungeeing it to the inside deck hatch handles. Hit a three-foot chop, and it swings out like an errant trapeze. As I mentioned a moment ago, I'm anal. A place for everything, and everything in its place—without the acrobatics, thank you. The simple placement of a full-length noodle across the face of the shelf was all that was needed to wedge and hold the ladder securely. As a matter of fact, we cruised from Riverhead, Long Island to Watch Hill, Rhode Island in some pretty nasty seas: four footers and building at certain points along the way. The ladder remained solidly in place as did the overhang protection.

The strip atop the doorframe comes off, of course, in order to close door. But you can bet your booty, mate, that item goes back on the second we open the hatchway, lest the one above it permanently serves as a stark reminder. Hence, single protection when heading out of the cabin; double protection when heading back inside. I'm sure you will find other uses for that versatile foam tube.

****

Nor'east Saltwater paid me $150 for the article. Not too shabby for a 900-word article, which took me little time to write and which I had fun doing. Although the magazine's guidelines call for 1,200 to 2,000 word submissions per article (flexibility mentioned for a bit of leeway in either direction), plus several photographs from which the editor may choose, there was just so much I could say about *Using Your Noodle* without forcing the piece with filler. I almost always write the maximum amount of words that is called for and would never have deviated from the norm by submitting such a short piece except for the fact that I maintain a good rapport with the editor. I first queried my editor (standard operating procedure), telling him precisely what I had and why I thought the article would be of interest to readers. He said he'd consider the article, which I e-mailed, along with several photos. He praised and accepted the piece. Had the editor not wanted the article, I would have then sent a query off to another publisher whose word count guideline was more in line with the length of my piece. You may be thinking, *Well, why didn't you just do that in the first place?* Well, for a couple of very good reasons. One: I wanted the piece published in *Nor'east Saltwater* because of a single individual whom I know reads each issue from cover to cover; the same person who, like me, cracked his head on that bloody @%##&* hatchway more than once. Two: I also wanted the article published in *Nor'east Saltwater* because it paid more. A line from playwright Arthur Miller's *Death of a Salesman* states, "Business is definitely business." I'm sure you would agree, that's using your noodle, too.

Bear in mind that most print magazines have a website, in which they include Writers' Guidelines or Editorial Guidelines. At times, the information may be imbedded in the site, and it is difficult to find. If so, go back to your Google search and type in: Writers' Guidelines or Editorial Guidelines, along with the name of the magazine. Also, it is important to query the editor by name instead of *Dear Editor*. There are freelance writers market lists available on the Internet, some of which are categorized by topic. That would be a good place to start. Also, there are online magazines known as eZines that pay writers for content; Google eZines for those listings.

You are not going to get rich writing freelance articles; however, you can make a few dollars and keep your name out there. As I spend most of my time writing novels, it is a nice diversion for me to turn out several outdoor articles a year. I tie the two endeavors together, often weaving those outdoor experiences through my fiction. Fodder if you will. If I spent more of my day freelancing articles, I could certainly write scores of pieces. But I don't want to turn what I enjoy doing into more work. I've learned to separate those pursuits: fiction/nonfiction. Balance is the key. To make a full-time job out of freelancing articles would subtract from my more serious endeavor—the novel. There are just so many hours in a day that one can devote to work and play, and playing in the great outdoors is of importance for both Donna and me. Try and find that workable balance in life.

BONUS FEATURE

Making Decent Dollars Writing ~ Plus Little-Known Reward-Reaping Benefits

In Lesson 12, you had a good look at how you can turn your area(s) of interest into dollars by writing for various publications. Well, from that vantage point, I'm going to tell you how you can reap additional benefits exceeding the monies you will make from your published pieces. Besides the satisfaction of being a paid published author, you can also enjoy certain advantages that go along with that privilege. Let's take a look at several examples.

You'll recall my mentioning having written several articles on kayaks and yak accessories—for which I was paid $300 for two articles from *Nor'east Saltwater*, and $355 for three shorter pieces from *The Fisherman*. Initially, I had written a query letter to the president & chief operating officer of Ocean Kayak, asking the gentleman to please make me part of their Professional/Media Discount Program, along with the promise that I would write articles promoting their fine products; mainly, their Ocean Kayak Prowler Big Game Angler model, which I coveted. It is important to note that I used my writing credentials with regard to *other* outdoors articles (mainly fishing articles) that I had published.

I received a response from the vice president and chief financial officer of Ocean Kayak, making me part of their Professional Discount Program, for which I received a nice discount on my kayak of choice as well as optional Prowler Package equipment. One of the items that I opted for was a pricey Hummingbird GPS 383c Chartplotter; that is, a fish finder/depth sounder. Also, a rudder system for the yak was on my *must have* list, along with several other accoutrements.

Keep in mind that I did not have to *promise* the company ink in order to be accorded the privilege of being made part of their program. Many of these businesses are happy to have you aboard. In the case of Ocean Kayak, the company banked on the fact that I would be a floating advertisement for their product. With my new Ocean Kayak Prowler Big Game Angler platform, I expected that I would be catching lots of bass and blues in some skinny waters inaccessible to larger vessels. Consequently, I knew that I would soon be doing several articles, showing off a large striped bass taken from the suds in their fine craft. Well, I certainly kept my promise, having written five articles on kayaks, promoting Ocean Kayak, along with other fine yaks.

In writing for such publications, while promoting a company's product, blatant advertising may be a no-no; in other cases, it may be permitted. Too, there are situations where the writer must be most tactful, doing a balancing act by making mention of competitors' products while subtly pointing to a favorite. The fact of whether or not a company is an advertiser in the publication for which you are writing can carry a great deal of weight in terms of an editor's latitude. The writer must be aware of the publications' requirements. It behooves you to pinpoint a publication's position before embarking on a full-fledged featured mission. This is easily accomplished by simply asking the editor of the publication precisely what their policy is concerning the company in question, leaving no room for guesswork or doubt. Once this is established, it's time to query the target company.

Let's take a look at one of my generic query letters that I send to prospective products companies, keeping in mind that at one point I only began, as some of you will, with a single credential to my name. My first outdoors article appeared many a year ago with the *1000 Islander and Rideau Lakes Voyageur* (Canada). The bulk of my outdoor articles for which I receive discounted products began in 2004. Again, as this is a general letter for purpose of example, I've addressed it to Dear Sir/Madam: However, I strongly suggest that you make it your business to identify the *name* of the proper party in charge of such a program, be it a marketing person or the president of the company. This can easily be accomplished by perusing the publication's masthead or Googling the Internet.

Robert Banfelder
141 Riverside Drive
Riverhead, NY 11901-2451
(631) 369-3192
E-mail: robertbanfelder@gmail.com

Dear Sir/Madam:

As an outdoors writer with hundreds of articles published to date, I would like to be a part of your Professional Media/Discount Program. The following paragraph will explain what I am prepared to do for your company.

As an award-winning novelist and the creator of a series of unique guides, one of which is titled *Fishing Smart for Salt Water & Fresh Water*, I have contributed articles to *The Fisherman, Nor'east Saltwater, On The Water, Hana Hou! The Magazine for Hawaiian Airlines, Big Game Fishing Journal*, and *New York Game & Fish* (to name but a few).

My website, www.robertbanfelder.com, has a complete listing of articles published to date. I enjoy the privilege of having been accepted by a good many Professional/Media Programs (or equivalent thereof). For example: Sales manager, **ArcheryTargetsdotcom**; Marketing representative for **Berkley Fishing**; Vice president of marketing, **Bushnell**, manufacturer of optical products; **Cabela's** promotion manager; Media director, **CAMX** Crossbows; **The Catch**, owner and manufacturer of fishing rod hook keepers; **Crimson Trace** Corp., makers of handgun laser sights; Marketing specialist for **EOTech** holographic laser sights; Marketing director, **Eposeidon/KastKing,** distributors of fine fishing gear; Marketing director, **Eppinger** Lures; **Hornady** communications manager; North America Marketing Manager, **Interlux**; President & CEO, **LL Bean**; Media relations manager of **Mathews, Inc.,** manufacturer of bows and archery accessories; Marketing director, **Mepps** lures; **Morrell Targets,** manufacturers of compound and crossbow targets; Marketing representative for **Muzzy** bowfishing; President and chief operating officer for **Ocean Kayak**, manufacturers of fishing and recreational kayaks; **Pettit Paint,** manufacturers of boat paints; Selected Angler Program Coordinator for **Pflueger/Shakespeare** reels; Owner of **Phase II Lures**, maker of wooden fishing lures; Marketing representative for **Plano** Mold, manufacturers of fine gun cases; President, **Porta-Bote** International, manufacturer of foldable boats; Customer sales and service representative for **Pyramid Air,** distributor of RWS air guns; Assistant to president of **Remington** Arms Company; **RIO,** makers of fly-fishing lines, leaders and tippets; **Shakespeare** Ugly Stik fishing rods; Marketing representative for **Shimano** fishing products—my having reviewed eight high-end spinning reels in a two-part series as well as their Lucanus Jig System; Blue Heron Communications, marketing representative for **Smith & Wesson**, **Pure Fishing, Thompson/Center Arms,** et al; Customer relations supervisor for **Subaru** America; Inventor and manufacturer of the **T.C. Gun Sling**; President of **Teeny**, Inc., manufacturer of quality fly lines; Rick Pope, president of **Temple Fork** Outfitters, makers of Lefty Kreh Signature Series fly rods; Blue Heron Communications marketing representative for **Thompson/Center Arms**; Director of sales and marketing, **Warne** Scope Mounts; **Yamaha** Motor Marketing Director, USA, manufacturers of Yamaha outboard engines; Communications coordinator for **Yamaha Motor** Corporation, USA; Creator of **Yamaha** outboard oil drain fitting and tube.

[Note: I have removed each company's representative name. Again, you should research the appropriate person and address your request directly to him/her.]

I would like to be accorded the same privilege via your company, purchasing and promoting such fine products through my article writing. Short of blatant advertising, I do get remarkable results.

I am a member of the Outdoor Writers Association of America, New York State Outdoor Writer's Association, Long Island Outdoors Communicators Network (founding member). I have been a past member of Eastern Flyrodders of Long Island, Loyal Order of Moose, Loyal Order of Moose Yacht Club, New York Sportfishing Federation (of which I was on the board of directors), and the Peconic River Sportsman's Club. Donna (my significant other) and I maintain a close relationship with a large network of community sportsmen and sportswomen.

 Once again, I do get outstanding results in promoting fine products and would like to do the same for your company through extensive article writing.

Please give this proposal your consideration. I look forward to hearing from you.

Sincerely,

Bob Banfelder

Award-Winning Novelist & Outdoors Writer
Cablevision TV Show Co-host, *Special Interests with Bob & Donna*
Member: Outdoor Writers Association of America
          NYS Outdoor Writer's Association
          Long Island Outdoor Communicators Network
          Trumansburg Fish & Game Club (Finger Lakes area)

www.robertbanfelder.com

****

    The long and the short of this business is that I received a 24.5% professional discount on my coveted Ocean Kayak Prowler Big Game Angler model, inclusive of the Hummingbird unit, transducer, anchor trolley system, paddle, deluxe seat, scupper stoppers, and Scotty Powerlock rod holders. Not too shabby. In most cases, on less expensive items, I enjoy a 40% discount or better. In some instances, I receive products gratis. However, as time went on, I requested products gratis since I had built up an extensive list of companies willing to send me their products free of charge in exchange for my promotional articles. I simply eliminated the word 'Discount' from my query to read: As an outdoors writer with hundreds of articles published to date, I would like to be a part of your Professional Media Program.

    By now, I am positive that you are saying to yourself, *"Hey, sure this guy is a shoo-in for a Professional/Media Discount Program because of his credentials."* Not so. Once again, be reminded that there was a point when I had but a single credential to my name, having written my first outdoor piece for a Canadian publication, yet I received professional consideration from a large retail merchandising company because I simply wrote a letter asking them for a discount. That was but one article. Years later, as I started writing novels, then editorials and articles concerning our criminal justice system, finally finding the time to write pieces about Donna's and my love of the great outdoors, I needed the *toys* and *tools* and a way to pay for them. Hence, beyond an occasional outdoor article, I make it my business to contact the corporate heads of companies, asking to be made part of their Professional/Media Discount Program, or equivalent thereof. In terms of reward, I look upon the monies I receive for writing outdoor articles as pieces of *silver*. The dividends I receive in terms of toys and tools are bars of pure *gold*.

    A 24.5% discount on a ticket item totaling $1,632.93, as the Ocean Kayak Prowler Big Game Angler Package offered (plus several options), is a decent discount. But that was just the beginning; 40% plus discounts are not unusual. I've received a much as 50% on both big and small ticket items. That's certainly something to write about, and that's exactly what I'm doing here. That's gold, guys and gals. Coupled with the monies you receive for writing related articles, the cost of many an item may be paid for completely. Also, keep in mind that as you go down the pike, it becomes an easier sell, both in terms of the pieces you are writing as well as the product(s) you are wishing to obtain. It's truly a win-win situation for all parties concerned; that is, the writer, the magazine or periodical publisher, as well as the product(s) manufacturer.

Let's up the ante and see how I made out querying a major international manufacturer and distributor of premium cycling and fishing equipment. My focus was directed toward the fishing arena, especially Shimano's rods, spinning and bait casting reels, with emphasis on the latter two items of interest. In order to reach all markets, Shimano offers retailers and consumers a range of low-priced spinning and bait casting reels to high-quality prizes that can be compared to a fine timepiece—both in terms of cost and refinement. Their high-end reels are superb; you pretty much get what you pay for.

As I am nearing retirement (Donna is already at that juncture), I decided to set aside some of my tired fishing tackle and equipment and purchase an assortment of new, high-quality Shimano spinning and bait casting reels. Donna, of course, wanted equal shares. Those of you who have been following my outdoor articles through the years know that Donna would rather shop at Cabela's than Cartier. Therefore, my comparison to Shimano's high-end reels as timepieces is an apt one—the jewel of my life standing over my shoulder as I perused the company's catalog. Candidly, the cost of my wish list was prohibitive. However, I had a game plan. I queried the company with my standard letter, informing them that I would write several articles covering their fine products. I was immediately made part of their Professional/Media Discount Program.

My first piece titled *Selecting Fine Lightweight yet Gutsy Saltwater and Freshwater Spinning Reel & Rods* covered four of Shimano's fine featherweights. I was paid $150 for the article, which became a two-part piece. My second article covered four of Shimano's larger spinning reels. The piece was titled *Selecting Major Weapons of Mass Destruction*, for which I received another $150 check. I was able to get away with virtually blatant advertising because I coupled Shimano's spinning reels to spinning rods manufactured by another company. There is no rule that says a rod and reel have to be paired from the same company. I offered the readership an affordable way to purchase a fine rod and reel outfit without breaking the bank, explaining that the consumer can buy a comparable rod for far less money by selecting a competitor's product; namely, Shakespeare's Ugly Stik. In a nutshell, it's a caliber Shimano reel coupled to a Shakespeare Ugly Stik rod that's the real deal, so it wasn't simply a clever ploy to get the editor to take these two articles because I only write and promote what I truly believe to be high-quality products for a fair price.

Next, PowerPro Braided Line was bought out by Shimano. I had written a piece titled *Monofilament versus Braided Line ~ Misconceptions and Modifications*, for which I received another $150 check.

In terms of fishing tackle, Shimano offers three unique but rather expensive jigging systems. What I initially thought to be a bit of hype by this Japanese company turned out to be precisely what the corporation claimed these systems were; that is, unusual, carefully crafted fish-catching lures. It's usually the fisherman who gets hooked by hype, but not in these three cases. Again, the lures are pricey terminal tackle fishing items, yet they are well worth the cost if you're a fishing fanatic—with an emphasis on the word *fanatic*. After briefly field testing these artificial lures, I stood convinced that there was nothing factitious about Shimano's claims; that is, the jigs' fish-killing abilities—for catching is believing! Covering but a single system, Shimano's Lucanus Jigging System, I wrote an article for *Big Game Fishing Journal*, receiving $350 for the piece. Nice catch. Yes? This exemplifies how one article can lead to another, netting me $800 for writing those four fun-filled topics.

Additionally, Shimano's Professional/Media Discount Program paid big dividends for Donna and me in terms of reduced prices on select merchandise: reels, tackle, braided line, clothing, footwear and other accessories. In most cases, those items were discounted between 40% and 50%. In a couple of instances, I received free merchandise (tackle and a rod) as a bonus for a fine writing job. Donna and I could not have afforded such high-quality items had I not been made part of Shimano's Professional/Media Discount Program. Shortly thereafter, I queried magazine publishers referencing writing articles covering Shimano's two additional jigging systems; that is, their Butterfly and Waxwing lures. The sky's the limit . . . or I should say that our bays and oceans provide bountiful fodder for future articles.

Although most of the product discounts that I received have fallen within the realm of fishing related equipment, I have also enjoyed the privilege of being made part of a Professional/ Media Discount Program pertaining to the area of firearms and accessory items noted in my general query letter to the aforementioned companies; namely, Remington Arms Company and Crimson Trace Corporation, manufacturer of handgun laser sights.

In the former instance, I was interested in Remington's Premier Model 11-87 semi-automatic 20 gauge shotgun, which had a manufacturer's suggested retail price of $827. With a standard query letter to Remington Arms, my cost, under the discount program, was $527, representing a 36.3% savings. As many a prudent shopper does not look to pay MSRP, you might feel that the $300 savings I posit here is overstated. However, when it comes to firearms, I believe you'd be hard pressed to find that gun on sale for more than 10% off of manufacturer's list of $827.

Next, with regard to Crimson Trace Corporation, manufacturer of handgun laser sights, I was after laser sights for two handguns: Donna's Smith & Wesson .22 caliber, Model 616, 10-shot revolver as well as my Smith & Wesson 9mm kurz/.380, Model PPK/S Walther, 7 shot semi-automatic pistol. The value of the two laser sights was $668, MSRP. The cost to me re these particular instances was zero dollars, admittedly because of my credentials writing outdoor pieces. Yes, it does take some years to build a reputation, but keep in mind that most of my expertise focused on fishing, while only a limited number of my articles reflected hunting and shooting as mentioned next.

Another outdoor activity I've covered is bowhunting. There came a point in time when I had to upgrade my 60-pound compound bow down to a 50-pound draw weight because of age (mine, not the bow's). Yes, age does have a habit of creeping up on you. The original bow, which I hunted with for fifteen years, was a Mathews. Quite candidly, I wouldn't own any other compound bow than a Mathews, innovators of the single cam bow. Although I am accepted as part of the Mathews Professional/Media Discount Program, pricing is and must remain confidential. That's their policy. What I can say is that I received a hefty discount, inclusive of two free components: bow rest and quiver. No sales tax, no shipping charge.

As a necessary accessory for the serious bow hunter/gun hunter, Bushnell manufactures a waterproof laser rangefinder, combining *both* a bow and rifle mode. This is a rather pricey piece of equipment that retails for $514.95. Being made part of their Professional/Media Discount Program, my cost was $292.00. That's a 43.3% savings.

At this point in time, both Donna and I are quite outfitted for retirement. That was part of our game plan. No, Donna does not hunt with me, although she has helped me track deer. With the emphasis on fishing, clamming and crabbing, all we really needed was a new boat and motor. Ready for the *pièce de résistance*?

Common sense would dictate that on a large luxury item, such as a boat and motor, the chance of receiving a hefty discount is slim. Once Donna and I narrowed our choice of boats down to a few, having decided on one particular engine, I set to querying companies to see what they could do for us—once again, with the promise of my giving the respective company some ink. One boat company offered me 4% off a promotion package in 2010, only to renege on the offer in 2011. However, Yamaha Motor Corporation made me a fair offer: 10% off the best deal I could find from a dealer. Done deal! In actuality, having been made part of their Professional/Media Discount Program, the communications and dealer education manager for Yamaha Motor Corporation, did a bit better than 10%. The bill of sale for the engine read $8,020; however, I received a check for $1,026.56. Yamaha had actually given me 12.8% off the price we paid for the engine.

Donna and I enjoyed a wonderful season on the water. When it came time to pull the boat, I contacted Yamaha to see if I could secure parts as part of their Professional/Media Discount Program, parts that I would need to service the engine. Pushing the envelope, I asked if I could also receive *spare* parts so that I would be set for the servicing the boat in seasons to come. The company sent me, at no cost, parts totaling $204.18, which will take me through two full seasons.

As I would, indeed, be bottom painting the hull down the proverbial pike, I thought it would be a good time to ask Interlux, North America's leading supplier of superior boat paints, if I could be made part of their Professional/Media Discount Program. The North America marketing manager for Interlux, e-mailed me explaining that they had no program as such but that she would send me two gallons of their best ablative paint that I had requested—free of charge! That's a savings of $467.18 when compared to a retail store's price; that is, $214.99 per gallon, times two, plus $18.60 tax for Interlux's Micron CSC antifouling ablative bottom paint. Boating is not cheap. Quality parts, paints and materials are quite expensive. However, if you can convince the powers that be that you say what you mean and mean what you say, meaning that you can be of service to such companies and that a working relationship is a two-way street, you will be rewarded for your efforts.

Now, for a little-known but big money-saving fact:

Donna and I saved a considerable amount of money by purchasing the boat and motor in Delaware. Comparing apples and apples, buying the package from a New York dealer would have cost an additional $3,200. The Delaware dealers' principals, along with their employees (mechanic and prep people), treated Donna and I quite professionally. We are quite pleased.

Additionally, the Delaware dealer's practice is to give the buyer a separate bill of sale—one for the boat and another for the engine. Therefore, when we registered the boat at the New York State Department of Motor Vehicles, we only paid sales tax on the purchase price of the boat, not the motor, saving an additional $692.53, which represents the tax we would have paid on the engine. This is all quite legal but not widely known. In truth, Donna and I almost missed this money-saving opportunity because some folks *believe* this is a no-no. A knowledgeable friend pointed out the *facts*, reminding us that when we registered our inflatable in New York, on which we place a small outboard motor, we are registering the inflatable, not the engine. You could remove that engine, buy another, place it on the inflatable, and nothing changes. Again, you are registering the craft, not the engine that propels the vessel.

It only becomes a problem when you purchase a boat and motor whereby the engine is an integral part of the craft, such as an I/O (inboard/outboard), or when the boat/motor is sold as a single package and the out-of-state dealer does not offer a separate invoice for the two items.

So far, our savings on the Delaware deal came to $4,919.09. But there's more! The boat came with a bunk trailer, representing $1,322.00, which we did not need as we already have a roller trailer. Our experience in New York has been that when there is a boat package deal (boat, motor and trailer), the dealer tells you that you *have* to take the trailer. "Put it on your front lawn and sell it," one N.Y. salesman told us. This was not the case at Midlantic Marine Center. The dealer would discount the cost of the trailer from the price of the package, saving us $1,322 plus $114.15 in New York State sales tax—less the cost of delivery from Delaware to Long Island, New York; i.e., $667. The grand total savings on our boat/motor purchase came to $5,688.24! Now, that's a whopping piece of change.

Could I write about this event and have it published in one of the magazines for which I write? Not likely because it would likely wind up having New York boat dealers lose business, and I'm not looking to do that. Let's face it. New York is expensive. I share this information with a select few—you the reader of this guidebook. I have already written articles in which I gave ink to the boat manufacturer (although I received no discount), Yamaha (whom, of course, I thank profusely), and Midlantic Marine Center. The hat trick was to cover the three mentioned companies without crossing the line into blatant advertising. The mere mention to include (with emphasis on the word *mere*) other boats and outboard motor companies was the key to success.

Once again, you do not have to *promise* to give a company ink in order to receive a professional discount. The fact that I freelance articles for various outdoors magazines usually suffices. However, I feel that I have a better chance of being made part of a Professional/ Media Discount Program and building a rapport by assuring a company that I can get them publicity and help promote their product(s). I offer to produce evidence of that claim by sending the president or media relations person copies of my published articles to prove past performance. This approach has rarely let me down.

The procedure can also work for you when querying a publisher/editor for an article you wish to submit. Informing the publication that you have recently purchased say a new kayak through the company's Professional/Media Discount Program immediately puts you in a different category. Your query should include the company's contact information: name of the person, his or her title, address and phone number. Apprising the editor, too, that you have caught some impressive fish on the yak and have high-quality support photos to accompany the piece will certainly pique the editor's interest. Before sending off the query, be sure of the publisher's guidelines, usually found on their website under Submissions. Follow the instructions to a T. If you cannot ascertain specifics such as required word count, et cetera, ask. Certain requirements may change from time to time.

Now, let's get down to the nitty-gritty, meaning what is absolutely essential to ensure success with regard to having a publisher respond favorably to your query letter, enjoying, too, the benefits of being made part of a company's Professional/Media Discount Program or equivalent thereof. Hopefully, both pursuits will follow favorably. What is of paramount importance to accomplish these ends is good writing and fine photos. Concerning the latter requirement does not mean that you have to take photos with a single-lens reflex (SLR) film or digital single-lens reflex (DSLR) camera coasting thousands of dollars. A good 35 mm digital single-lens reflex camera will make life easier than a film camera. Today's SLR cameras are more than sufficient for the job. When Donna is photographing pictures for my articles, she uses a Fuji Finepix S1800 12-megapixel, 18x wide-angle zoom lens, purchased for $150, which is adequate for my purposes. However, if I were photographing, say, roses for a prestigious horticulture magazine, I would have to upgrade to a more suitable, more expensive DSLR camera. Digital cameras come with instructions on how to upload the photos to your computer. You then save and store the photographs in a My Pics folder. When you need to submit a photo, simply attach it to your e-mail. *Voilà*! No need to make back-and-forth trips to the photo store to develop film. Convenience and cost savings alone should convince you to go this route.

I trust that this guidebook has provided you with the necessary writing skills to accomplish your goals.

Discover your niche, write about it, proof your work aloud, then find a publisher —further capitalizing on your abilities by querying appropriate companies, asking them to make you part of their Professional/Media Discount Program or suchlike role. You'll pay far less for products than you would ordinarily; occasionally, you'll receive such items gratis. Follow this advice, and you will both make and save money, in addition to calling yourself a paid professional writer.

It's been my pleasure in presenting this material, and I wish you the best of luck —keeping in mind that for the most part you make your own good fortune in this world of ours.

Postscript:

There are several venues for having your fiction or nonfiction manuscript published. Most every crime-thriller writer dreams of being as successful as James Patterson, Jeffery Deaver, Thomas Harris, Sandra Brown, David Baldacci, or Kathy Reichs, but it is a hard road. Not impossible, but difficult.

Let us first consider securing a literary agent. Literary agents all have their favorite genre. The Literary Market Place (LMP) reference book, available at your local library, is the best way to find a literary agent that favors your genre. Once you have a list of agents that you feel will suit your work, go to the Internet and note their submission guidelines. Additionally, you must check out the agent as to his or her reputation and the authors they represent. A reputable agent should be a member of the Association of Authors' Representatives, Inc. The organization's member database is available online. A website that you may also use to see if your agent list is legitimate is AgentQuery.com. But you should also dig deeper into their history. Online writers' forums, such as AbsoluteWrite.com, are helpful in this regard. It is very important that you follow submission guidelines, as literary agents are inundated with queries and have little time to deal with queries that do not follow their requirements. The agent will be assessing your writing skills, so be sure to write a dynamite query letter that will pique his or her interest. Outstanding sample query letters that successfully secured a literary agent may be found on the Internet. Remember that most literary agents would require that your manuscript be complete before you query. In the event that a literary agent responds to your query and wants to see your work, again follow the guidelines for submission. Note that the agent may indicate that your partial manuscript be submitted in the body of the e-mail. Most literary agents will accept queries and manuscript submissions via e-mail. Once the literary agent agrees to represent your work, he/she will reach out to publishers. Be wary of any literary agent who requires payment to read your manuscript. If you are lucky enough to secure a legitimate literary agent to represent your work, you are on your way to becoming a successful published author.

If you decide to forego the process of trying to secure a literary agent, or if you have been unsuccessful in your efforts, you can try querying small publishing companies. The same process holds true with small publishers as it does with literary agents. The legitimate small publisher makes its money by selling your book. Again, you should not pay to have your manuscript read. Avoid those folks like the plague. Do your due diligence regarding small publishers and learn their method of royalty payment. It is advisable to have a literary attorney review the contract before you sign.

Should you decide to self-publish, there are various companies through which you can have your manuscript formatted into a book. Lulu and Createspace are two companies that will do this for you. You can format the interior of the book yourself, or you can have the company do that for you for a fee. If you want to format the book yourself, you can use a free software program available on the Internet called Open

Office Writer. Cover design (see Lesson 9) is especially important, so if you are going to create your own cover, do some homework. There are numerous tips on the Internet on what makes a good cover. The same holds true for titles. Createspace is owned by Amazon, so your book will be automatically available on the Amazon website within a few days. Of course, you can hire someone to do all of this for you, no differently than our newfound company, Broadwater Books (www.robertbanfelder.com). Notwithstanding, with patience and perseverance, you can learn how to format your book's interior, create a cover design, and upload your book for publication. The printing of your book will usually be on demand as folks order copies, so you will not have to store thousands of books in your home. You can also upload your book in e-book format. Kindle Direct Publishing, also owned by Amazon, is one venue. Self-publishing companies also offer marketing services for a fee. When you self-publish, be aware that *you* will have to do all of the marketing and promotion of your book.

There are a few good reasons why folks self-publish. One of them may have to do with age. I had asked Frank Mundus (world famous shark fisherman discussed earlier), why he self-published his last nonfiction book (*Fifty Years a Hooker*), especially after having his first book published in 1971 by McGraw-Hill. After telling me that I should know the answer to that question, he began to explain:

"Bob, you know how long it takes to go through the process of securing a literary agent then have that agent find a publisher. I'd be dead and buried before that ever happened." And Frank was, oh, so right. Frank was 83 and passed away only three years after *Fifty Years a Hooker* was published.

Food for thought, folks.

om/pod-product-compliance